Experiences in Science
for
Young Children

Experiences in Science
for
Young Children

donald b. neuman

DELMAR PUBLISHERS
COPYRIGHT ©1978
BY LITTON EDUCATIONAL PUBLISHING, INC.

LIBRARY OF CONGRESS CATALOG CARD NUMBER: 76-53185
ISBN: 0-8273-1642-9

Printed in the United States of America
Published Simultaneously in Canada by
Delmar Publishers, A Division of
Van Nostrand Reinhold, Ltd.

Donald B. Neuman

Jeanne M. Machado-Consulting Editor
Elinor Gunnerson-Early Childhood Education Series Editor

DELMAR PUBLISHERS • ALBANY, NEW YORK 12205
A DIVISION OF LITTON EDUCATIONAL PUBLISHING, INC.

Preface

There is a growing demand for information on the teaching of science in Head Start, day care, nursery, and kindergarten classrooms. This information can reach teachers in two ways: directly through local and national early childhood organizations; or through adoptions at university, junior college, and technical schools for classes designed to train early childhood educators and aides. Teachers are aware of the possibilities for science with preschool children. They are keenly interested in introducing a systematic presentation of science skills and concepts to their children. However, they need information on what to teach and how to teach it. EXPERIENCES IN SCIENCE FOR YOUNG CHILDREN addresses each of these needs.

The text is divided into three major sections. Section 1 consists of seven units that provide basic theory about science teaching, child development, and the meaning of science. Based on this theory, the author then describes his program of sciencing. Sciencing is a combination of concepts and investigative activities related to science, taught in either a formal, informal, or incidental manner. Each unit includes behavioral objectives, theory as well as practical application (suggested activities), summary, and review questions to evaluate students' comprehension. Section 2 consists of fifty-three science-related activities that have been classroom tested with three- to five-year-old children. Each activity has an introductory statement of purpose, behavioral objectives (what the child should learn from the activity), list of materials, procedure, and comments. These activities are divided into categories that relate to the information provided in unit 3 of the first section. Section 3 consists of useful information for implementing sciencing activities. This information includes a discussion of basic science topics; how to find and prepare materials; list of supplies; and readings for teachers.

The author, Donald B. Neuman, received his MA in General Science and PhD in Science Education from Michigan State University. He is both a certified elementary school teacher and college instructor, currently teaching Curriculum and Instruction, and Science Education at the University of Wisconsin. Dr. Neuman specializes in the teaching of science to young children, and his vast experience includes service as an early childhood teacher-aide; co-authorship of the text, *Creative Activities for Young Children;* and active participation in a number of professional organizations, including the National Science Teachers Association, Wisconsin Society of Science Teachers, and National Association for Research in Science Teaching.

Other books in the Delmar Early Childhood Education Series include:

- Teaching Young Children — Beatrice D. Martin
- Early Childhood Experiences in Language Arts — Jeanne Machado
- Administration of Schools for Young Children — Phyllis Click
- Early Childhood: Development and Education — Jeanne Mack
- Creative Activities for Young Children — Mary Mayesky, Donald Neuman, and Raymond Wlodkowski
- Experiences in Music for Young Children — M.C. Weller Pugmire
- Home and Community Influences on Young Children — Karen VanderVen
- Early Childhood Education in the Home — Elinor Massoglia

Contents

SECTION 1 WHAT SCIENCING IS ALL ABOUT

SECTION 2 SCIENCING ACTIVITIES

SECTION 3 SUGGESTIONS FOR TEACHERS OF YOUNG CHILDREN

A current catalog including prices of all Delmar educational
publications is available upon request. Please write to:

Catalog Department
Delmar Publishers
50 Wolf Road
Albany, New York 12205

Or call Toll Free: (800) 354-9815

Section I What Sciencing Is All About

unit 1 an introduction to sciencing

OBJECTIVES

At the end of this unit the reader should be able to

- State a definition of sciencing.
- Tell the meaning of the term process and explain how process is different from product.
- Describe how sciencing allows teachers to identify a variety of "best" pupils.

Most people have experienced a science course at some time during their education. Perhaps high school biology stands out most clearly in their minds. Some may recall junior high general science or the study of rocks and minerals in the fourth grade. Whatever the course or level, the word science for them probably means memorizing facts and formulas, repeating names and measurements, and remembering symbols and equations. Many people tend to remember science as seeming difficult to understand. Science for those people was a frustrating experience. Some remember it as being boring, consisting mainly of sitting still, listening to lectures, and answering difficult questions on complicated tests.

Is science such as this an appropriate topic for young children? Should three- to five-year-olds be made to "suffer" through a science program? If it is like the one many people have "suffered" through, no! The kind of science that most adults have experienced is not appropriate for young children.

Science is not just a body of facts to be memorized and then repeated on written examinations. It is not just a series of experiments to be performed in a laboratory. Science is an activity that few people have experienced. Real science is almost totally unrelated to the science people remember from their school experiences.

THE MEANING OF SCIENCE

What is science in its truest and fullest sense? One way to discover the answer is by working out the solution to a simple problem. As this problem is being solved the full meaning of science will become clearer. Thoughts and actions taken to find the answer should be analyzed.

> Problem: Determine what is inside a wrapped gift box without opening the box. Anything can be done to the box except unwrapping it and looking at its contents. It can be shaken, tilted, jiggled, pounded upon, listened to, and smelled. A magnet, magnetic compass, or stethoscope can be used on it. The box may be X-rayed, fluoroscoped, or put in a compactor. The problem is to find out what is in the box without being able to look inside.

To solve this problem, one's imagination must be used because there is no box to directly examine. Therefore, the following facts are provided for consideration. These facts are the result of many experiences with this gift box experiment in which people were given the chance to actually manipulate (handle) the boxes in any way they desired. They too were asked to: (1) name the object in the gift box and (2) tell what this has to do with the meaning of science in its truest

sense. This is the information that was discovered from examining the gift box:

- *Fact 1:* When the box is shaken back and forth there is the sound of a single object rolling back and forth.
- *Fact 2:* When the box is shaken to the left or to the right there is the sound of a single object sliding to the left or to the right.
- *Fact 3:* When the box is shaken there is the sound of a single object striking the top and the bottom of the box.
- *Fact 4:* A magnet does not attract the object.
- *Fact 5:* Placing a magnetic compass on the gift box and moving it about the surface shows no effect on the needle of the compass.
- *Fact 6:* If a stethoscope is placed on the box there is still no sound at all. By tilting the box to the left, a loud sliding sound is heard followed by a clunk as the object strikes the side of the box.
- *Fact 7:* An empty box identical to the gift box weighs eight ounces. The wrapped box weighs nine ounces.

- *Fact 8:* There is no distinctive odor on or around the box.

- *Fact 9:* By squeezing the box very tightly so that the top and bottom go together slightly, the object can be partly trapped. The object then seems to roll in a semicircle when the box is moved back and forth. When the box is moved from left to right and to the left again, there is no sound at all.

What is the object? Sift through the facts. Use logic and common sense. To aid in finding the solution, here are two additional clues:

- *Clue 1:* The object is a common one, recognized by most people when they see it.

- *Clue 2:* The object in its present shape is not living nor has it ever been alive.

What is the object in the small gift box? What evidence is there to support this guess? What else might the object be? Why might it be that? While attempting to identify the object, record each idea on a chart like the one shown in figure 1-1.

It is the answer to the question, "What does this activity have to do with the nature and meaning of science?", that is of major importance. The answer can provide a direction for planning and carrying out science activities with young children. It can help in making decisions about the selection of materials, the amount of time given to science, and the kinds of involvement children should have.

	Name of Object	Evidence
First Guess		
Second Guess		
Third Guess		

Fig. 1-1 Chart for gift box guesses.

What is science? There is no absolutely right or wrong definition. There are, however, more accurate and less accurate meanings for the term science. From the gift box experience one might have come to realize that science is a series of answers to questions. What is at the core of the earth? What is the universe like beyond the range of a telescope? What is in the gift box? Science answers many questions. These answers (facts, principles, and laws) are called the *products* of science. Product, in other words, is the information turned up or created by scientists. Products answer the question: What is science about?

But science is more than just answers to questions. Science is a way of looking at the universe. It is a way of investigating. It is the way in which a person goes about making discoveries in hopes of turning up new, and perhaps better, facts. Science helps answer such questions as: How can one find out? How can one be certain?

The ways in which scientists carry out their work are called the *processes* of science. Processes answer the question: How does one find out?

Most people are aware of the *what* part of science. Fewer know about the equally important, and in some ways more important *how* of science. In other words, science in its truest and fullest sense is a combination of two things: product (what) and process (how).

> Science is both information about the natural and man-made world and skill in discovering that information.

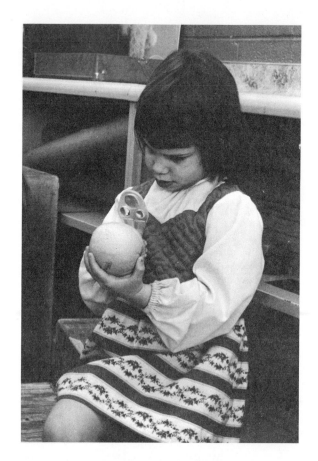

SCIENCE AND CHILDREN

When one thinks about science for children, the definition given above is very appropriate. Science is defined as a mixture of process and product. This mixture changes as the age, maturity, development, and physical abilities of children change. Teenagers, for instance, are able to deal with knowledge gained from hearing or reading about science. They have the maturity and experience to deal with a science mixture that places more emphasis on product and less emphasis on process. Nine- and ten-year-olds learn best when science activities stress a fifty-fifty blend of process and product. Three- to five-year-olds can best deal with science activities which place more emphasis on process than on product.

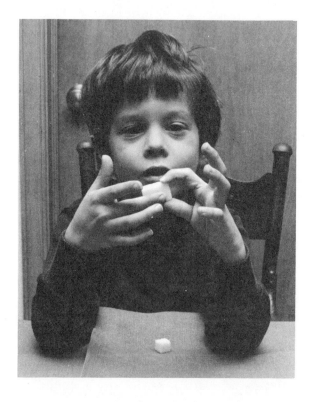

THE MEANING OF PROCESS AND PRODUCT

For younger children the ability to process science-related information is more important than the information itself. Several examples can help clarify this point.

Baking a cake involves both a process and a product. The product is the finished cake. But in order to have a successful finished cake, a baker must go through a process. This process includes (1) reading a recipe, (2) identifying and gathering all the proper ingredients, (3) gathering the needed pans and utensils, (4) mixing the right things in the right amounts at the correct time, (5) setting the temperature of the oven accurately, (6) reading the time when the cake is placed in the oven and when it is to be removed, and (7) mixing a good frosting. If any of the steps in the process are not properly applied, the cake is likely to be a failure. There can be no successful product without understanding and skill in applying the process.

Scientists use both process and product, too. For instance, a scientist may study distant stars and try to interpret messages being sent from them. An instrument called a radio telescope is used to observe the electronic sounds from outer space.

A scientist must be able to (a) make careful and accurate observations of the message being received, (b) collect and analyze the information, (c) develop some possible explanations (called *hypotheses*) about the source and meaning of these messages, (d) test the hypotheses, (e) draw conclusions, and (f) communicate the results to other scientists so that they can test these findings for accuracy using their own instruments. The information found about the distant stars is the product. The ways in which the information is discovered are the processes. As in the case of baking a cake, if a scientist fails to apply one or more of the processes correctly,

the result may be a failure (poor products or no products at all). Thus, a scientist and a baker, a baseball player and a tailor, an X-ray technician and a ballerina must learn and understand the processes used in their work. Once they are able to correctly use the processes, they are ready to apply them to produce some worthwhile products.

It should be remembered that science, like other areas of human work, consists of processes and products. Science as an activity designed for young children has most of its emphasis placed on the process aspects. Some, but much less emphasis is placed on the development of science-related knowledge.

WHAT IS SCIENCING?

One of the first statements made in this unit is that "science is an activity that few people have experienced." Most people have been exposed to some basic facts and concepts of science. They have memorized a body of knowledge. That is not, however, an appropriate method for teaching science to three- to five-year-olds. Science for young children should involve the children in physical activities in which they work with materials. In this way, children can be helped to become better observers, better communicators, and better classifiers. It is desirable to involve children in science activities that are challenging, creative, and fun.

In order to indicate science that is appropriate for young children, a new term is used in this text. This term is *sciencing.* Sciencing is a much better word for the purposes of this text. It is a verb – an action word. Science, on the other hand, is a noun – a thing. Sciencing emphasizes the actions of the child; children develop the ability to apply process skills. In science, the learning of facts is stressed. Sciencing involves children in full and active participation in a variety of experiences. In science, children can be passive spectators to the activities of others.

Children should have a variety of materials and equipment available to them. They should be encouraged to use these things. There must be freedom for them to move and openness in which to operate. Children must have the chance to make discoveries, and a wise, understanding teacher to help them clarify those discoveries. Sciencing is an activity that provides children with these opportunities because it motivates children to action.

THE IMPORTANCE OF SCIENCING

There are a number of good reasons for involving children in sciencing. Children are interested in the world around them. They need to develop worthwhile hobbies. However, there is one reason that is of more immediate value to them than any of the others mentioned. Moreover, teachers and parents of young children are deeply involved in this rationale for sciencing.

Bright = Verbal?

Ask some teachers of three- to five-year-olds to list the four brightest children in their current group. Then ask them to list the four children who are most verbal. In most cases the two lists contain the same names. Many teachers perceive the best readers and/or the most verbal children in their group to also be the best all-around pupils.

Is this accurate? Are the best readers, speakers, or listeners in a class really the best all-around pupils? This perception on the part of many teachers takes on new meaning in the light of some recent research. It has been found that a teacher's opinion of the worth of a pupil (who is the "best" one) can have a great impact on the child's school performance. That is, if a teacher believes one pupil is a high achiever (whether the teacher's perceptions are based on accurate or

faulty data) that youngster is likely to fulfill the prophecy and be a high achiever. However, if a teacher believes a child to be less able, this too becomes a self-fulfilling prophecy. Teachers can convey to children their feelings about the child's worth or lack of worth without being aware of their actions. The children tend to respond accordingly.

If teachers consider their best pupils to be the ones who are most verbal, how does this thinking influence pupils who are not highly verbal? What are their self-concepts like? There are children who are quite bright and are able thinkers but are not verbal. Some of them are even nonverbal (those who do not speak very well or very often). Evidence indicates that there are many such youngsters. Are bright children who do not read or speak well ever identified? If so, how? When? Is there some way in a school's curriculum that children can show their intellectual skill if they do not speak or read well? In most schools, these bright but verbally slow children are never recognized.

If teachers judge a child's worth mainly on reading and other verbal skills, they often fail to recognize many of their bright students. They overlook children whose abilities are equally valuable to society but are less highly prized by teachers. Many teachers, for instance, do not recognize the importance of logical thinking. They do not place much value on being able to deal with abstract ideas. Some are not concerned with the worth of problem solving skills or the importance of being able to stick with a problem. A student who may be a genius in solving abstract problems can go unnoticed by teachers whose main concern is preparing a child for reading or bringing everyone up to the grade level in reading.

Sciencing Activities

Ways must be found to recognize bright students who lack verbal abilities. That is,

teachers must identify activities in which a child who is not verbally skillful can find success. School programs must be made up of activities that are designed to encourage pupils to show their wide variety of talents. The problem is to discover these types of activities and then to recognize their value.

Sciencing is one of the activities that fulfills this need. Sciencing gives children the chance to demonstrate their skills. It does not force children to talk about those skills.

7

Children who are investigating are learning by doing, not just by speaking or listening. Thus, it is possible to discover bright, but nonverbal children by observing them during sciencing activities.

These nonverbal children are rarely recognized for their skills. However, when they are discovered, teachers should let the children know they have been recognized. If the child's feeling of self-worth can be increased, then it is likely that additional successes will follow.

SUMMARY

Sciencing is activity. It involves some simple methods and materials related to science. Sciencing activity encourages children to investigate and develop new skills. It is activity that gives a child a way to show off skills that are not related to verbal ability. Sciencing is activity designed to challenge young children and help them to realize that learning in a school setting can be fun.

> The answer to the gift box problem (page 2) is: a thread spool.

unit 2 sciencing and child development

OBJECTIVES

At the end of this unit the reader should be able to

- Describe how physical development patterns of children influence the teacher's choice of activities for those children.
- Explain the difference between fixed and interactive intelligence.
- State and describe two social-emotional needs of children that can be influenced by adults.

Nancy is three years and five months old. She stands three feet, two inches tall and weighs thirty-four pounds. Her eyes are blue and her hair is blond and combed into pigtails. She can lift and carry a large cardboard container. She can button her coat but she is unable to tie her shoes. She is able to catch a large rubber ball and throw it underhand.

Nancy does not speak unless she is spoken to. Her answers are usually short and consist of one syllable words. She pays close attention to stories that are read to her. She does not seek out books or spend time looking at pictures. She tends to play by herself, usually with the same doll.

Nancy does not smile a great deal. She cries easily and often sits alone in a corner sucking her thumb. She tries to avoid games that force her to play with other children.

Now meet Rodney. He is three years and seven months old. He stands three feet, one inch tall and weighs thirty-two pounds. His eyes are brown and his hair is black. He can lift large boxes, build block towers that are five blocks high, button his coat, and zip a zipper. He can catch both large and small rubber balls and can throw a small ball overhand.

Rodney tends to be a quiet child. He has a limited speaking vocabulary. He does not enjoy being read to, although he does spend as much as fifteen minutes per day looking at pictures in books. Rodney tends to be a leader in play activities. He selects the toys or games for himself, and others usually join him in what he is doing.

Rodney is generous with other children. He likes to share and makes other children feel comfortable in his presence. He laughs easily and seems to enjoy a wide variety of activities. Rodney is usually willing to try a new game.

Finally, meet Glenda. She is three years and six months old. She stands three feet tall and weighs twenty-nine pounds. Glenda has brown eyes and black hair. She can lift and carry large objects, but cannot grasp very small things. She cannot button her coat, zip up a zipper, or tie her shoes. She can neither catch nor throw a ball. She can roll a large rubber ball along the ground.

Glenda speaks clearly and well. Her vocabulary is considered remarkable for a three-year-old. She loves to be read to and is able to recognize simple words. She spends much time in the reading corner. She looks at pictures and repeats stories out loud that she has learned by heart. Playing with toys does not seem to interest Glenda. She has no favorite toy or doll.

Glenda prefers being alone in her world of words and stories. When the teacher insists, she will play with other children. Glenda does what she is told and seems to be very cooperative. The only time she takes a lead in an activity is when the activity involves words.

What do these three children have in common? Are they typical three-year-olds? Is there such a thing as a typical three-year-old? What can be learned about educating children from these three youngsters?

This unit is designed to try to answer these questions. In particular, questions about the physical, intellectual, and social-emotional growth of children are examined.

A basic position taken by the author involves differences among children. Nancy, Rodney, and Glenda are different from one another. They are different in height and weight. They do not have the same degree of large and small muscle control. They have different amounts of interest in word-related activities. They each relate differently to the children around them. While Rodney seems self-confident, Nancy is shy. Glenda is less sociable, but not shy.

Because children are so different from one another, it is difficult to make firm statements about their likes or dislikes; how they act or don't act; how they look or don't look. For every child who seems to fit an expected mold, at least three others do not.

PHYSICAL CHARACTERISTICS OF THREE- TO FIVE-YEAR-OLDS

How tall should a four-year-old girl be? At what age should a child be able to tie his shoes? When should a child be able to throw a football? These questions have no real

answers. Tallness or shortness may result from the genes with which one is born. It may be influenced by the food one eats or illnesses one has had. Coordination, too, is tied to a combination of inherited characteristics and external experiences.

Physical characteristics of boys and girls at any given age are different. Two boys or two girls of the same age may have very different physical characteristics. Differences between boys and girls of the same age are the result of basic physical growth patterns of the sexes. Differences between two boys or between two girls are the result of individual differences in growth patterns among all children.

For example, one might collect information on large numbers of boys who are four years and three months old.

- How tall are they?

- How much do they weigh?

- How tall a block tower can they build?

- Can they button a coat or tie a knot?

Was the number of boys sampled large enough? Was a wide variety of social and economic classes represented? Were many geographic areas used? Then some averages could be found. Based on these averages, a "typical" four year and three-month-old boy might be described. In a similar way, boys and girls of other ages can be described.

However, these are averages. The number of "typical" boys or girls found in a group would be small. In fact, there may be no "typical" boys or girls in a particular group.

In a study carried out several years ago at the Institute of Child Welfare, a large amount of information on boys and girls was collected. Children's physical and mental growth patterns were followed over a long period of time. Efforts were made to describe a "typical" three-year-old boy. The task was found to be almost impossible. Those who conducted the study concluded that each child has a unique growth pattern.

Physical skills, in particular, follow a unique growth pattern. There are many factors that influence a child's physical development, such as genes, food, illnesses, home environment, life experiences, and other variables. Muscles must be used in order to develop and grow strong.

Because each child develops at a different rate, all three-year-olds cannot be expected to perform the same physical actions. Two different four-year-olds will not have the same amounts of muscle control or strength. Some five-year-olds have good hand-eye coordination. Others are very weak in this area.

Each child must be seen as an individual. The only way to make accurate statements about a child's physical skills is to study that child. Moreover, that child should be studied over a long period of time. Only then can reliable information about a child's physical state be determined.

Thus, a teacher must realize that many factors affect a child's physical development. The teacher must see each child as an individual, growing and developing at an individual rate. Then a teacher can:

- Plan activities which provide for the variety of physical skills that are likely to be found in any given group of children.

- Recognize that the needs of a variety of children can only be met by a variety of activities.

- Realize that the physical growth of children can be influenced by the activities planned and provided for them. Give children a chance to use large and small muscles. Know where to start and how to proceed.

INTELLECTUAL CHARACTERISTICS OF THREE- TO FIVE-YEAR-OLD CHILDREN

Some psychologists believe that a child's intelligence is determined before birth. The genetic material provided by each parent is thought to be the major determinant of a child's intelligence. The child's intelligence is said to be *fixed* (unchanging during life). If this is true, then little of what a child experiences in life can influence his basic intelligence.

Others say it is the experiences of the child that determines the child's IQ. The genetic material provided to a child by his parents is of little importance. If this is true, then all of a child's experiences determine the child's intelligence. Using this theory, if all children have the same experiences, all children should have the same IQ.

Both of these positions are extreme and few people take either of the extreme positions. Many more speak of an *interactive* intelligence. That is, the material with which a child is born plus the child's experiences interact (work together) to form the child's total intelligence. For example, consider the inherited capacity of each child to be

that child's "water glass." Some children are born with a very large "glass." Others are born with a smaller "glass." Life experiences, especially those of the first five years, represent the water in the glass. To illustrate this: Child A is born with an intellectual potential equal to a ten-ounce glass. Child A has experiences during his first five years equal to five ounces of water. For the purposes of this discussion, five ounces of water in a ten-ounce glass equals an IQ of 100.

Child B is born with a slightly smaller intellectual potential — an eight-ounce glass. However, child B has life experiences during her first five years equal to six ounces of water. Assume that the six ounces of water in an eight-ounce glass equals an IQ of 120. See figure 2-1.

Thus Child A, with a higher potential, may test out at a lower level on an IQ test

Child	Inherited Intellectual Potential	plus	Experience	equals	measured IQ
A	10-ounce glass	+	5 ounces of water	=	100
B	8-ounce glass	+	6 ounces of water	=	120

Fig. 2-1 Intelligence equals inherited capacity plus experience.

than Child B. Had the glasses of both children been filled to capacity, Child A would have tested out at a higher IQ than Child B. The life experiences of Child B enabled her to overcome the fact that she had been born with less potential than A.

Many people do not feel the IQ test is a valid measure of intelligence. Their argument is that too many decisions have been made about the relative worth of a child by measuring IQ. In addition, IQ tests tend to favor verbal and middle-class children. Every person, however, has what can be called thinking ability. This involves the abilities to reason, to think abstractly, and to evaluate and solve problems. Different children have different amounts of these abilities. If these abilities are called intelligence, then various children have different levels of intelligence. Life experiences (especially those in the first five years of life) are key factors in the development of intelligence. The analogy of the water glass and the water applies to intelligence as well as to measured IQ.

Much research has been carried out over the past twenty years in an effort to relate early experience and intelligence. Evidence points strongly to the fact that the amount and the kind of early experiences are crucial to a child. Lack of experience or lack of a variety of experiences limits a child's intellectual growth.

THE WORK OF PIAGET

Probably no one has contributed more to the understanding of intellectual development than Jean Piaget. Piaget is a Swiss biologist, psychologist, and philosopher. He has studied the intellectual growth of children for approximately fifty years.

Piaget has theorized that children go through a series of intellectual stages — one stage at a time. Each stage is marked by

certain intellectual behaviors on the part of the child. In one stage a child's thinking may be illogical as compared to adult thinking. At a later stage the child is able to think in a more logical way.

Piaget states that two important keys to intellectual growth in children are experience and social transmission. *Experience* is defined as children's physical contact with the world. Children must physically examine their world using all of their senses. They must change things from one form to another. Intellectual growth cannot occur by merely being told about things. *Social transmission* relates to verbal exchanges between children and adults. Children need to talk about their physical experiences with others in order to clear up their thinking. They need to try out ideas on adults — ideas that begin with their

physical experiencing of the world around them. By means of experience and social transmission (and physical maturation) children develop the ability to think. They grow intellectually.

Thus, a child's intellectual growth is directly related to the child's experience. Children who have a variety of experiences early in life are more likely to approach their maximum intellectual potential than those who have few experiences. Moreover, experiences in which a child physically examines the world around him add greatly to intellectual growth.

Activities in school contribute to the intellectual growth of a child if the activities:

- Are related to a child's abilities. They should not be too difficult or too easy.

- Do not require the child to think like an adult. People who develop activities must know that a child's logic is different from that of an adult.

- Help a teacher learn more about each child's thinking ability.

- Contribute to the total amount and quality of each child's experience. Activities should help children understand the world around them. An opportunity should be provided for children to discuss their findings and clarify their thinking.

SOCIAL-EMOTIONAL CHARACTERISTICS OF A THREE- TO FIVE-YEAR-OLD CHILD

In the study of children, a third area of growth involves social and emotional development. General patterns or stages of physical and intellectual growth have been identified. Stages of social-emotional growth can be examined in a similar way. For example, as an infant, the child and his mother appear to be a single unit. Children cannot separate

themselves from their mother's presence. The child needs the mother and, in turn, the mother needs the child. At about the age of two, children become interested in other children. However, children do not relate to each other as people but as things. That is, a child treats another child as a toy or a piece of furniture. Other children are things to be pushed or knocked over or moved about. Somewhat later — about the age of three — children begin to interact with each other as they compete for toys or other objects. They begin to sense other children as being more than just toys. Soon this leads to the development of playmate relations. Finally, children

reach a stage where they see each other as individual people worthy of respect and love.

In the process of learning to deal with other children effectively, each child begins to develop a feeling of self. Some children view themselves as unsuccessful in relating to other children. They lack confidence in their own abilities as social beings and as performers. They feel inadequate and behave accordingly. Children who are insecure with themselves become cautious. They are afraid to express joy or enthusiasm when things are going well. Successes may seem just temporary.

Insecure children may be equally afraid to show frustration and hostility. They prefer to cover up outward emotions. In that way they are not likely to further destroy their social positions.

In contrast, children who are confident in themselves feel secure. They know that they have been successful in their relationships with others in the past. They feel certain that they will be successful in the future. Small setbacks do not emotionally destroy these children. They are confident and emotionally healthy.

Thus, children who are confident in their social abilities tend to be confident in their intellectual abilities, too. Children who see themselves as successful performers in one activity tend to view themselves as successful in other activities. Teachers, parents, and other adults must therefore:

- Place children in situations where such basic needs as security and companionship can be satisfied.

- Plan activities that bring children together in close working relationships to help meet these needs.

- Help children begin to view themselves as socially skillful people. Once they feel socially capable, they will expect other skills to be within reach, too.

SCIENCING AND YOUNG CHILDREN

It is clear that all children have certain skills and certain needs. The kind and amount of skills differ from child to child. Basic needs are shared by all children. Other less basic needs differ in kind and amount from child to child.

A person who works with children and plans activities must be aware of these skills and needs. In general, two factors must be considered when planning children's activities. They are:

- What can a child be expected to do at a given point in his development? Activities should not be too demanding. They must not, however, be so easy that a child learns nothing new.

- What can activities contribute to a child's growth? Activities should help a child's physical development. They should provide for a child's intellectual growth — both in the developing of skills and the learning of knowledge. Activities should help children develop social skills and a feeling of self-worth.

Sciencing, as a series of activities, is described in detail in the following units of this text. Certain key points made in this unit should be kept in mind when reading the other units.

- Are sciencing activities designed in a way that recognizes the uniqueness of each child?

- Do sciencing activities contribute to the physical, intellectual, and social-emotional growth of children?

- Do sciencing activities provide children with a wide variety of experiences?

- Are sciencing activities designed to help children feel successful?

If activities are to help each child grow in some positive way, the answer to each question should be yes. It is easy to lose sight of basic objectives as one works with children from day to day. It is therefore important to have some basic beliefs about children and their needs. It is equally important to think about and act upon those basic beliefs as one plans activities. Sciencing

activities can contribute to the growth of children.

SUMMARY

Children are unique in terms of their abilities, needs, interests and growth rates. Three main areas of development are physical growth, intellectual growth, and social-emotional growth. Experiences influence a child's growth in all three areas of development. If children do not have a chance to use small muscles, they are not likely to develop small muscle coordination. If children are not stimulated intellectually, they are not likely to develop higher-order intellectual processes. If children are not placed in social situations, they are not likely to develop social skills.

There is a certain amount of interaction among the three areas of development. Physical growth can influence intellectual growth. Intellectual growth can affect emotional growth. Emotional growth can influence physical growth. Each area of development thus affects the other areas.

Activities designed for children must meet the basic needs and skills of children. Sciencing is a series of activities that does this.

SUGGESTED ACTIVITIES

Observe a group of children in a classroom setting. Look for the following things:

- Is there any activity in which all children participate? Do all the children seem to be equally interested in the activity? Is there evidence that some are bored? Are there any children who are frustrated?

- Study the children in terms of their physical abilities. How many can:

    a. Build a block tower two blocks high? Four blocks high? Six blocks high?
    b. Pound a nail into a piece of wood?
    c. Turn a screw into a piece of wood?
    d. Dress a doll in an outfit with snaps? With buttons?
    e. Put on and button their own coats?
    f. Zip a zipper?
    g. Throw a 15-inch rubber ball underhand? Overhand?

- Study children in terms of their knowledge skills. How many can:

    a. Count to five? Count to ten? Count to twenty?
    b. Identify one to five letters of the alphabet? More than five letters?
    c. Name the eight primary colors?
    d. Identify the sound of the first letter of two to five words?
    e. Identify and name the shapes circle, square, rectangle, and triangle?

- How many children spend time observing objects and investigating on their own? How much time do they spend doing this? Identify ways in which these children do their investigating.

- Study the social roles children play. Select one child to observe. In a thirty minute period:

    a. How many children does the child play with? Speak to?
    b. What evidence can be seen to determine whether this child is a leader or follower?
    c. Does this child seem to prefer working alone or in a group? What role does the child play in group activities?
    d. Does this child appear to be successful in performing activities?
    e. At any time did this child physically fight with another child? Verbally argue with another child? If either answer is yes, what caused the problem?

- During a thirty minute period, how many minutes are spent in which:

    a. The teacher does all of the talking?
    b. A child responds to a teacher's question?
    c. A child asks a question?
    d. Two or more children are speaking?
    e. No one is talking?

f. Children are working with close adult supervision?

g. Children are working without close adult supervision?

- Write a paper based on observations made, interpreting the meaning of these observations. What can be said about children? What is the role of the teacher? What kinds of activities seem most appropriate for the children?

REVIEW

A. Complete the following by choosing the best answer.

1. Physically, all children develop

   a. At the same rate.

   b. At the same rate for the first three years of life, then at different rates.

   c. At different rates.

   d. At different rates for the first three years of life, then at the same rate.

2. Coordination is determined by

   a. Experience.

   b. Genetic inheritance.

   c. General health.

   d. A combination of all three factors (a, b, and c).

3. Intelligence is

   a. Based only on experience.

   b. Based only on genetic inheritance.

   c. Based on an interaction between nature (genes) and nurture (life experiences).

   d. Not based on genetic inheritance at all.

4. Fixed intelligence is said to be

   a. Related to a person's ability to repair things.

   b. Related only to physical matters.

   c. Determined at conception and unchanged after birth.

   d. Constantly changing.

5. IQ tests favor

   a. Children with few life experiences.

   b. Children who cannot talk.

   c. Children who are polite.

   d. Children who are highly verbal.

6. A child who feels secure

   a. Also feels confident.

   b. Also is very strong and muscular.

   c. Has learned to accept failure.

   d. Has not learned to accept failure.

7. Piaget believes that children

   a. Are all alike.
   b. Go through stages of thinking one stage at a time in a fixed order.
   c. Go through several stages of thinking at the same time.
   d. Can think logically just after their third birthday.

8. Insecure children may be afraid to

   a. Make friends.
   b. Show frustration.
   c. Show hostility.
   d. All of the above.

B.   Short Answer or Discussion

1. Define the following terms:

   a. Interactive intelligence
   b. Fixed intelligence

2. Name two social-emotional needs of children that can be satisfied in school-like activities.

unit 3 formal sciencing

OBJECTIVES

At the end of this unit the reader should be able to

- State the meaning of formal sciencing.

- Define the term process and name four basic processes.

- List four content topics in sciencing and describe why each is important for young children to know or to experience.

Children for whom sciencing is intended are undergoing a period of remarkable change. They are growing physically and developing fine motor skills at a rapid rate. These children are also going through a period of rapid intellectual growth. Their level of understanding and thinking abilities are increasing quickly. They are experiencing growth in self-confidence. They are also developing the ability to turn away from the self and to share with others.

Growth patterns and interests vary from child to child. Many factors influence each child's ability to function at any given time or in any given activity. Therefore, when planning a program of activities for young children one factor must be constantly kept in mind: *variability*. Each child is unique in terms of growth rate, personality, specific needs, and interests. Yet all children share an important trait with other youngsters. They need to become successful human beings. They need to see themselves as able performers in some area of endeavor.

Each adult who works with a young child must learn to recognize this need. Each adult, whether a parent, teacher, relative, or friend

CHILDREN ARE:	—THEREFORE—	ACTIVITIES SHOULD BE:
Unique in terms of their skills and interests.		Sufficiently varied to meet a variety of skills and interests.
In need of seeing themselves as successful performers.		Success-oriented. Success at some level must be built into activities.
Unique in terms of their growth patterns and life experiences.		Varied in type, length, difficulty, and emphasis.

Fig. 3-1 Sciencing activities are designed to provide children with a variety of experiences and a feeling of success.

of the child, must provide chances for the child to succeed. The activities that are described in this unit reflect a concern for children's variability. They also reflect a desire to provide for children's success. Figure 3-1, page 20, summarizes the philosophy underlying the activities to be discussed in this unit.

OVERVIEW OF SCIENCING

Trained teachers, interested parents, and other helpful adults feel that certain topics and experiences are important for children. Children have special interests that result in a desire to learn about certain topics or have various experiences. The natural and man-made world also provides topics and experiences for children. Each of the three factors (adult wisdom, children's interests, and the world around us) has contributed its share to the program called sciencing.

Adult wisdom has resulted in the aspect called *formal sciencing.* Here a teacher plans activities, gathers materials, and motivates children to learn both the "how" and the "what" of science. Specific objectives are identified. Materials designed to help children reach the objectives are provided. Children are encouraged (but never forced) to participate. Outcomes are evaluated. Formal sciencing is one part of a total program.

In the second part, called *informal sciencing,* children's interests are recognized. The teacher's role is minimal in this aspect of the program. A wide variety of materials are organized and provided for children. These materials are made available on an as-needed and as-wanted basis. Children are made aware of the existence of the materials and encouraged to use them. What they learn from the materials they learn on their own or by working with other children. In every way, this second aspect of the total program is as its name implies, informal. This phase of sciencing is described in detail in unit 4.

Sometimes nature provides a special learning opportunity. A sudden downpour on a sunny day may result in a rainbow. A diseased elm tree may be cut down near one's school or home. A death in the classroom aquarium or a birth in the terrarium may lead to many questions which need answers. Incidents such as these are not planned. They just happen. Alert adults can help children take advantage of these opportunities in a

third aspect called *incidental sciencing.* This phase is also described in unit 4.

FORMAL SCIENCING

A class of eighteen five-year-old children has just returned from a period of outdoor play. As they enter their classroom, they notice that a series of containers has been placed at each of six locations. Immediately they move to each of the locations and discover that there are five containers at each place. They further notice that the contents of the containers at one location are the same as the contents at each of the other locations.

The teacher gives a brief explanation about the six stations and the containers at each station. The children are asked to use the ingredients found at one of the stations to make frosting for cupcakes which the teacher has brought. If they make a frosting that they do not like they can discard it and begin again. The children are asked to keep track of the ingredients they use and about how much of each. When their frosting is made, they can each frost a cupcake and eat it.

The children quickly and noisily put on their sciencing smocks and proceed to gather ingredients, spill powdered sugar, drop a cup of water, and mix the cherry juice with strawberry flavoring. But each child also manages to prepare a tasty frosting, spread it over the top of a cupcake and enjoy it. As the children are busy mixing and tasting, the teacher moves about speaking to individual children. After most of the children have made a frosting and finished their cupcake, the teacher asks the children to meet in a corner of the class to share what they've learned.

"What have you discovered?" asks the teacher. One child noticed a change in

color. Another speaks of the bad taste which results from mixing cherry, chocolate, and strawberry flavors together. One child noted that when too much water was added to the powders, the frosting was not thick. But by adding more powdered sugar, the frosting got thicker.

"Oh, you mean you were able to change a liquid to a solid by adding the solid to the liquid?" asks the teacher. "I guess so," returns the child.

By this time it is evident that some children are tired of this activity. Several asked if they could try to make another frosting and were told they could if they clean up any messes they make.

Is this formal sciencing? Has learning really taken place? The answer to both questions is yes. This is a formal activity designed to build the child's concept of change. It also provides an opportunity to help children use the process skills of observing and classifying.

The activity is a formal one because the teacher selected the topic. The teacher gathered the materials and introduced the topic. The results were discussed with individual children, small groups, and possibly with the whole class.

Formal sciencing is made up of the two segments of science presented in unit one. These are (1) the facts of science — the *what* and (2) the investigative skills of science — the *how*. The facts of science are the *products*. The investigative skills are called the *processes*.

PROCESSES USED IN FORMAL SCIENCING

For the purposes of this text, *process* relates to skills needed to carry out investigations. These are skills used by scientists, children, or anyone who is trying to learn about the world around them.

Several processes could be described here. However, some are too complicated for young children to use. Therefore, only four of the skills are given. These skills are called *inquiry process skills*, and the process phase of sciencing. They are the easiest to understand and the most important of the skills which children should gain from sciencing. The processes are:

> Observing — using the five senses
> Classifying — sorting objects
> Quantifying — comparing, counting, and measuring
> Communicating — sharing findings

THE IMPORTANCE OF PROCESSES

Processes are used in many ways almost every day. For example, a person planning dinner for a family uses each of the four processes (very often without realizing it). That is, this person observes, classifies, quantifies, and communicates about the preparation and eating of the food.

Observing

A person must observe what the family eats. It is senseless to cook something that no one enjoys. One way to find out what the family enjoys is to observe them as they eat certain foods.

Do they eat with vigor?

Do they finish all the food and ask for more?

Do they compliment the cook?

Do they push the food around on the plate to make it look like they have eaten?

Observing these things will help a person find out what a family will eat and what they will not eat. Knowing what the family will eat helps make a person a better cook.

Classifying

Dishes, silverware, pots, and pans are usually sorted in a kitchen. Dinner plates are found in one place in the cupboard. Saucers are in another place. Forks are separated from knives and sauce pans are kept apart from pie tins. If the dishes and silverware were not carefully classified in some way, problems could develop. Therefore, a good cook tries to classify the dishes, pots, and silverware in the kitchen.

Quantifying

How are numbers used in cooking? Food amounts are measured. The time needed to cook various items is determined. The size of containers is evaluated. The cost of various cuts of meat or of beans or potatoes is considered. Quantifying thus plays a central role in planning and cooking a meal.

Communicating

"This tastes great!"

"I think you used too much salt."

"Not this again!"

"You are really a great cook."

Some kinds of communication may bring a smile or a frown to the face of a cook. It is by means of communicating that one learns about the success or the failure of a meal. Sometimes no words have to be spoken. A smile or a frown tells the whole story.

It should be clear that the four processes can be used to help a person plan a family meal. Being alert and knowing about these

processes can help improve the quality of the meal. Not using the processes can have the opposite effect.

Many examples similar to that of meal planning can be given to show that processes are widely used — almost every day by everyone. Processes are used in planning a budget, buying new clothes, planning a trip, or helping a friend solve a problem. In each case some observations must be made. Some things or ideas must be classified. Quantifying must be done. Communicating must be carried out. The ability to use these processes is useful in solving problems of day-to-day living.

A CLOSER LOOK AT THE FOUR PROCESSES

An important objective of sciencing is to help children understand and use the four basic processes. In order to help them reach this objective, people who work with children must first understand the processes themselves. This section is designed to help the reader gain an understanding of each process.

UNDERSTANDING THE MEANING OF OBSERVING

How many observations can be made about a common object like a sugar cube? (A life saver or other piece of candy could also be used.)

Gather the following materials:

- Several lumps of sugar, sugar cubes, life savers, or other hard candy
- A small cup of water
- A spoon or a fork
- A book of matches
- Some scratch paper and a pencil
- A ruler

Using any or all of the materials, try to make twenty observations about the sugar or candy in ten minutes. Write down each observation on a piece of paper. Do not read any more until the observations have been made.

Some of the observations that people make involve measuring the size of the cube or candy. They taste the object. They hold a match under it to see if it burns or melts. They touch it to see if it is rough or smooth. Mostly, they use their eyes to look the object over.

Using the eyes is one form of observing. There are other senses that must be used to make good observations. The senses of smell, touch, taste, and hearing must also be used.

In the observations made about the sugar or the candy, did any involve the sense of smell? Was the sense of hearing used? If not, try to make some additional observations using all five senses.

Observing is the most basic skill a child can develop. A good observer sees, hears, smells, tastes, and feels things with great skill. Good observers relate to the world around them with greater accuracy and greater depth. One who is a good observer often becomes a better reader and possibly a more successful adult.

The keys to observing are: (1) the knowledge that observing involves all five senses; (2) the willingness to use all of the senses and to apply the needed effort to make accurate observations; and (3) the physical ability to use the five senses in order to make careful observations. Through experience the ability to observe can be developed and can become a valuable learning tool.

Understanding the Meaning of Classifying

How many ways can a deck of playing cards be sorted? It can be sorted by color, suit, number or picture. It can be sorted by all of these methods. Sort a deck of cards into categories of your own choosing. Try as many ways as possible.

Sorting or classifying is used by many people in many ways. Primarily, it is used to help make sense out of things that would otherwise be unorganized. For instance, what would a kitchen be like if the dishes, silverware, pots, and pans were not sorted in some way? What would a supermarket be like if groceries were thrown all over the place? What if books were just spread out on the floor in the public library? How could an item be found in the classified ads in a newspaper if they were not organized in some logical way? In dresser drawers, aren't clothes classified and placed in certain parts of the dresser?

It is important that children and adults learn to classify. They must learn to sort objects on the basis of observable characteristics. Most important, they must learn that there are many ways to classify a set of objects. For example, a group of books can be arranged alphabetically by title, or by topic, or by author. Books can also be classified on the basis of the color of the cover, or on the basis of size. Some arrangements work better than others.

Understanding the Meaning of Quantifying

What is the temperature today? How long is that table? How high is this ladder? Are there more yellow marbles or blue marbles? Who can run faster, Bessie or Jane? Which piece of cloth is roughest? Which is

smoothest? Who is first in line? Who is second? How many blocks are there on the table? Which shoes are largest? Which child is the shortest? How many girls are in the group?

All of these are examples of quantifying — using sizes or numbers in some way. Measuring the size of an object, comparing two objects to see which is larger, counting, and arranging in a numerical order are all forms of quantifying.

> Think about buying a new automobile. Write down all the ways quantifying can be used in deciding which car to buy. Think of at least ten ways to use quantifying.

Quantifying is an important skill for children to develop for a number of reasons. First, it helps them observe, classify, and describe objects more accurately. Second, it is the basis for later learning in mathematics.

The numerals children use in sciencing are the ones they will use later in addition.

Understanding the Meaning of Communicating

How does one person get information to another person? How can someone make sure that the meaning of a message is clear? It is not always easy.

> Try to describe a shape to a person who cannot see it. Do not let the person see it until it is described. Have the person draw the shape as it is being described.
>
> Try to describe a maple leaf to a person who has never seen one. Tell a person who never saw a submarine how it looks.

One often hears that an argument was the result of a lack of communication. Parents and teachers sometimes cannot communicate with children. Children sometimes cannot communicate with adults. Many children do not communicate with each other.

In some cases, people cannot communicate because they lack the right words to describe or explain a certain situation. Other times, communication is blocked because people lack the necessary experience in describing or explaining a particular object or situation.

Thus vocabulary and experience are basic to good communication. Language development and reading readiness are closely tied to the ability to communicate effectively.

It is very important that children have experiences about which they can speak. However, communicating is not limited to verbal forms. Drawing is also a form of communication. Facial expressions and acting out (without using words) are also forms of communication.

Regardless of the way children express themselves, it is important that they be encouraged to communicate. They may express feelings, describe an object, or explain a situation. They may use words, gestures, or pictures. Whatever form is used, children must learn to communicate ideas and feelings. Above all, they must learn to communicate with accuracy.

CONTENT USED IN FORMAL SCIENCING

In addition to the four processes described, some basic content is also stressed in formal sciencing. The content material that makes up the formal phase of sciencing is carefully chosen. Topics are selected that meet the following standards:

The knowledge must be useful to young children. A topic is useful to a child if the information learned can be used in many ways and in many areas. It is not productive to crowd a young child's mind with facts and more facts. Some information is, however, useful and necessary. A child can use the information again in many areas of study.

For example, a child can be taught to identify twenty kinds of insects on sight. This can be very exciting for some children. However, for most children, the value of that knowledge is questionable. On the other hand, a child can learn that some insects look alike. Others look very different from one another. The understanding that all objects (whether they are insects or electric clocks) are alike in some ways and different in others is a very useful piece of knowledge.

BASIC SCIENCE THEMES	EXAMPLES
Objects are made up of basic (smaller) units. Properties of objects result from the make-up of the basic units.	Books are made up of pages. Sentences are made up of words. Water is made up of droplets. A flowering plant is made up of flower parts, leaves, a stem, and roots. Each part has identifying characteristics.
Basic units come in three forms: solids, liquids, and gases.	Woods, metals, cloth (something that has a shape of its own) are solids. Water, oil, alcohol (something that takes the shape of the container in which it is placed) is a liquid. Air, oxygen, carbon dioxide (they have no shape) are gases.
Objects change over a period of time.	Bread turns moldy. Ice melts (if the air around it warms up). Gelatin sets (if the air around it cools off).

Fig. 3-2 Sciencing topics provide children with basic science understandings.

Topics used as the basis for sciencing activities are useful topics for young children.

The knowledge must be related to basic science information. Each topic that is chosen for sciencing is related to one of several basic and broad science themes. In order to understand how sciencing activities relate to each other one must be aware of the science themes that are used. Figure 3-2 names some themes used in sciencing and provides an example of a topic related to each theme.

Topics used as the basis for sciencing activities provide children with important science understandings.

While acquiring sciencing knowledge children should develop skills. Young children need a chance to develop large muscle coordination. In addition, they benefit from experiences that help them develop the smaller muscles. Hand-eye coordination is also important. Finally, children develop a readiness to move their eyes from left to right (the way they do when they learn to read). Each of these skills can develop and grow as children participate in sciencing activities. As children handle large and small pieces of equipment

they develop muscle control. As they pick up and study objects carefully their hand-eye skills grow. As they arrange objects from left to right or from top to bottom (on a table, on a chalkboard, or on a floor) prereading skills develop.

There are two steps to skill development. First, children must be actively involved in the learning. They must physically handle objects — move them around. They must arrange and rearrange the objects. Second, the topics selected must lend themselves to active child involvement. They must be topics in which children can work and learn with relative ease. They must be topics for which simple materials and equipment can be found.

Topics used as the basis for sciencing activities help children develop important skills.

The knowledge must be discoverable. Whatever children learn in sciencing must be information they can discover for themselves. Children do not benefit from being told all of the answers. They learn by doing. Therefore, the topics that are most valid for young children to learn are those that children learn for themselves. For this to happen, topics must be easy to understand. They must be learnable by means of direct investigation. Topics must require actions by the child that are within the child's abilities. They must require only simple, easy-to-find materials. Topics should be carefully selected so that they help children discover and understand the world around them.

Topics used as the basis for sciencing activities are discoverable by children.

TOPICS USED IN FORMAL SCIENCING

Four criteria for selecting sciencing topics were stated in the preceding section. They were:

- Knowledge is useful for children.
- Knowledge is good, basic science.
- Knowledge helps build useful skills.
- Knowledge is discoverable by children.

Four content-related topics are suggested in this text. Before selecting these four topics a wide number of possible topics were used with young children. After several years of these tryouts, a large number of topics

were dropped. Some were found to be too difficult for the children. Others were too slow moving to hold children's interests. Some led children to discover useless information. In the end, four topics proved able to meet each of the four criteria.

Topic 1: Describe objects in terms of their properties. Is a metal chair made out of aluminum, cast iron, or lead? What kind of clothing should a person wear on a very hot day? Should motor oil or water be added to fruit flavored powder to make a cool drink? In order to answer questions such as these a person must know something about the

materials being discussed. What are the characteristics of aluminum and lead? What properties of oil would make it unsuitable for mixing a cool drink?

In order to study the world around them children must learn to recognize basic characteristics of objects. These basic characteristics are called *properties*. Some properties of objects include temperature, color, texture, size, bounciness, viscosity (thickness of a liquid), shine, and smell.

It is important that children learn to recognize properties of objects. A child who can identify properties can study objects in greater depth and with more meaning. Children can talk about their findings as they study changing objects or similar objects. The child can develop a mind set that emphasizes investigating — a willingness to study the properties. Science understanding is based on the ability to describe objects carefully, accurately, and fully. This can not be done unless one is able to name the basic properties of objects.

The ability to examine objects in order to identify their properties is basic to additional learning and discovery. Children should be given many opportunities to examine and compare a wide variety of objects. The basic goals of these experiences are to learn the names of properties and to be able to identify the properties when they are encountered.

Topic 2: **Describing similarities and differences among a variety of objects.** How is a robin like a blue jay? How are they different? How is a leaf from an elm tree like that of an oak and how are they different? How is the sound made by a trumpet similar to that of a clarinet? What are the differences? Objects, sets of objects, and classes of objects can be compared. Comparison is usually based on properties of objects such as color, shape, sound, and other factors.

The availability of objects and sets of objects to be compared is almost limitless. Children's shapes can be compared. The design of classrooms can be examined and compared. The sizes of rubber balls or colors of flowers can be compared. How are they alike? How are they different? How does one know? What is the evidence? Valuable learning takes place in a classroom or home where children are challenged to study and compare.

Of particular value in these activities is the broad range of correct answers that exist. A child's idea of what is similar and what is different can grow in an atmosphere of freedom. If a child believes two objects are alike in some way and can justify this feeling, the child's interpretation must be accepted. The child is correct and has been successful. It is not the adult's expected answer that gains acceptance. It is the child's ideas that become important.

It is also important for children to develop a mind set for looking at objects in

terms of similarities and differences. When they later look at letters such as R and P, they will attend to how they are alike and how they are different. O and Q, B and P, D and O are other examples of similar appearing letters. Thus, these activities can serve as prereading, skill-building experiences.

Topic 3: **Describing properties of common solids, liquids, and gases.** What are solids? Is ice a solid? Is a piece of satin or a marble a solid? What is a liquid? What do liquids have in common with one another? How are solids and liquids alike? How are they different? Are most common gases colorless and odorless? How does one know that air is a gas?

All of these questions are basic to science and many answers can be developed in sciencing. Children can begin to develop a concept of solid, liquid, and gas by having experiences with these three kinds of matter. The young child may not be able to define the terms. However, the child can develop an understanding of what a solid is, what a liquid is, etc.

Children can learn that solids have properties such as hardness, rough or smooth texture, and different colors. They can observe that some liquids feel oily to the touch and some have a bad odor. They can feel air pushing on the inside of a paper bag or balloon while they push on the outside.

It is important for children to learn about solids, liquids, and gases as concepts. This knowledge helps children deal with their environment. It helps them express their feelings and state facts they observe. To know about the states of matter is to know basic science. To study and learn about matter is a basic goal of sciencing.

Topic 4: **Studying objects as they undergo change.** Combine some cabbage, tomatoes, a carrot, some celery, and a green pepper in some water in a blender. Turn the blender on for one or two minutes. What has happened? Can the carrot be separated from the mixture after the blending process is complete? Combine sugar and sand and thoroughly mix the two substances. Can the sugar then be separated from the sand? How is the first blending different from the second? Place some oil, water, and liquid starch in a tall thin glass container. Watch the three liquids separate into three layers. Shake up the

mixture. What has happened? What happens after an hour? After twelve hours?

Some things can be combined and then returned to their original form. Other things, when combined, form a new substance. The properties of the new substance may be unlike any of the original materials. Furthermore, there is no way to separate the new product into its original materials. Still other materials or objects change when their position is slightly altered. Rearranging some wires leading from a dry cell can change the wiring patterns in a circuit with startling results. Changing the position of one child in a group can result in some obvious group differences.

It is important that children develop an understanding of the term change. However, the only way they can really understand the term is to experience change. They must see what happens when a new fish is introduced into an aquarium. They must see and feel what happens to jello after it is removed from a moderate oven.

ORDER OF PRESENTATION

Usually, children first experience the process skills of sciencing. They then apply each of the skills to a body of sciencing content. In other words, a child should experience activities in which observing and communicating skills are stressed. Then those skills can be applied to a body of information — such as change. Thus, a child may observe and describe how a piece of banana changes over time, when placed in a covered baby food jar.

The order in which children experience process skills and content is not absolute. However, some orders make more sense than others. Here is one suggestion:

Children experience activities related to observing

then

Children experience activities related to communicating

then

Children experience activities related to classifying

then

Children experience activities related to quantifying

then

Children apply each of the processes to experiences involving the following content:

Describing properties
Describing similarities and
    differences
Describing solids, liquids, and
    gases
Studying changes

SUMMARY

Formal sciencing consists of activities designed to develop children's skills in investigating the world around them. They then

apply those skills to the study of a body of information. Skills used for investigating are called processes. The processes stressed in sciencing are observing, classifying, communicating, and quantifying. The knowledge to which the process skills are applied includes naming properties; describing similarities and differences; identifying solids, liquids, and gases; and studying changes.

SUGGESTED ACTIVITIES

- For each object, make as many observations as possible in ten minutes:
  - (a) A match
  - (b) A tree
  - (c) An insect
  - (d) An ice cube

- Determine the way a supermarket has been organized. That is, how are the various food items classified and arranged?

- Find a picture of a squid. Using the picture, write an accurate description of the squid in one hundred words or less. Give the description to a friend and have the friend draw the squid using your description.

- Make a list of simple, easy-to-find objects that can be used by three- to five-year-old children to study change. Compare the list with others.

- Measure the length and width of a table using materials other than a ruler to make the measurement. How many ruler substitutes can be found?

- List all of the words that can be used to describe each of the following objects:
  - (a) A hollow rubber ball
  - (b) An inflated balloon
  - (c) An ice cube
  - (d) A drop of cooking oil
  - (e) A piece of wood and the sawdust from that piece of wood (use sandpaper)
  - (f) A strand of human hair

REVIEW

A. Complete the following by choosing the best answer.

1. Formal sciencing is planned by

   a. Children.
   b. School administrators.
   c. Parents.
   d. Teachers.

2. Whether to participate in informal sciencing activities is up to

    a. The child.
    b. The school administrator.
    c. The parents.
    d. The teacher.

3. Incidental sciencing takes place

    a. Every day.
    b. When something special happens.
    c. When the teacher thinks it should.
    d. When parents think it should.

4. Formal sciencing consists of

    a. Process skills.
    b. A body of knowledge.
    c. Attitude development.
    d. A combination of process and knowledge.

5. The process of quantifying involves

    a. Using numbers, measuring, and counting.
    b. Much discussion.
    c. A need for special science equipment.
    d. None of the above.

B.   Short Answer or Discussion

1. What does the term process mean?

2. Name and describe two of the four processes.

3. Name three content topics basic to formal sciencing.

4. State an order in which process and content can be introduced to children in formal sciencing.

unit 4 informal and incidental sciencing

OBJECTIVES

At the end of this unit the reader should be able to

- State the meaning of informal sciencing.
- Name and describe five topics that can be used in informal sciencing.
- Describe two situations in which an incidental sciencing session would be appropriate.

Enter a classroom of young children. The children have been busily engaged in activities for about thirty minutes. In one corner, several children are pounding nails into some boards. Two children are playing grocery store and three more are slapping finger paints on paper. They appear to be enjoying themselves. Suddenly something happnes. One of the nail pounders loses interest in pounding nails into boards. Two of the finger painters are now painting each other.

What has gone wrong? Nothing has really gone wrong. What has happened is that the children have become tired of the activity in which they were engaged. This is natural. But what can children do when they tire of class activities? Is there a variety of options open to them? Do they feel free to participate in the various options? Are the optional activities interesting? Are they challenging?

This unit is designed to describe a series of activities that meet children's needs for variety, interest, and challenge. Described are informal and incidental sciencing activities — when to use them, and how to use them.

INFORMAL SCIENCING

Children bring a variety of interests, experiences, skills, and intellectual abilities to every situation. Some children need careful direction and close supervision; others function best in an atmosphere of openness and freedom. Some have long attention spans; others cannot concentrate for more than two minutes at a time. Many children like to play with animals, while others are fearful of all living things.

To meet the needs of a variety of children, a variety of activities must be made available to them. Informal sciencing provides part of the answer to this need for variety. It is meant to be an optional activity. Children can decide whether to participate or not to take part in an activity. They may participate for as long or as short a period of time as they wish.

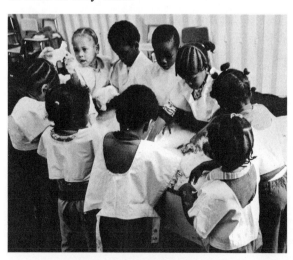

Objectives of Informal Sciencing

Many activities for young children are designed to reach certain goals. Informal sciencing is not such an activity. Children do not have to learn any specific facts from the activities. They may, however, learn a great deal of information. Children can become familiar with interesting materials, or they may prefer to avoid the materials. Any of these options is acceptable.

Informal sciencing is not meant to be forced onto any child. Hopefully, the children will want to use the materials provided; they will find the materials exciting; and they will learn something from their experiences.

Under these circumstances, only general objectives are appropriate. These include the following:

Informal sciencing should stimulate a child's curiosity. Children are interested in the world around them. If given a chance to explore that world in some way, their natural curiosity is challenged. They learn to feel free to explore and to enjoy probing for answers. A feeling develops that curiosity is not a bad thing. They learn to accept their natural feelings and to feel good about them.

Informal sciencing should encourage a child to use free investigation methods. Much of a child's world is discovered by a process of free investigation. Some call this trial-and-error learning. The child tries something to see what happens. If the results are rewarding, the child has learned something. Even if the results are not rewarding, the child has still learned something. If interest continues at a high level, the child may try something else, and then something else, until a desired result is achieved (or until total frustration is reached). Some of the most valuable science discoveries are made through free investigation. Many great findings are the result of trial-and-error investigation.

Children should learn to use simple, science-related equipment. Sometime in most children's schooling they are likely to use a balance. They will probably wire a simple circuit or study a vibrating object such as a tuning fork. They will read a thermometer and use a magnifying glass. What better way is there to get them started than by having simple materials made available at as early an age as possible? In the right kind of class climate children can investigate freely and manipulate the materials in ways that make sense to them. No one will tell them what to do or how to do it. They will find out for themselves.

Children should be able to develop a feeling of personal success. A child must know that materials are available to use. Children should also know that whatever is learned from using those materials is fine. Many things can be learned from a set of materials, if enough time

is given to use them. In this way, children are likely to discover that they have been successful while using those materials. Success in sciencing is a state of mind. If one feels successful, one has been successful. And success in one activity is likely to breed success in other activities.

SELECTING TOPICS FOR INFORMAL SCIENCING

A few general rules should be remembered as topics for informal sciencing are chosen. One set of rules applies to equipment and materials. Another set relates to the topics themselves.

Equipment and materials should be:

- Easy to find and inexpensive (or free).
- Easy for children to put together and use.
- Easy to store and easy for children to reach.
- Attractive to the children (colorful, clean, unbroken).
- Safe to use.
- Useful in helping children discover new ideas or rediscover old ones.

Topics with which materials are used should be:

- Reasonably safe for children to work with. (Children should be warned about the hazards of sticking wires into electric sockets, for example.)
- Useful for helping children make many discoveries. One should not try to anticipate exactly what a child will discover in a given experience. Often some unexpected but positive discoveries are made by a child playing with materials.
- Interesting enough to attract children. They should also be the kind that hold children's interests.

- Varied so that the largest possible number of children find something of interest to explore.

- Self-instructing. That is, the materials should lead children to make discoveries with little direct teacher help.

SCIENCING TOPICS

One should understand the goals of informal sciencing and know the basic ways in which topics are selected. It is important to know the children in a particular classroom — their interests and abilities. Then it is possible to decide if a topic is useful for their particular situation.

Several topics are very useful in a large variety of situations. These topics are discussed briefly in this section. A more detailed description of each topic is provided in Section 3 of this text.

Basic Electricity

Using simple materials such as a battery, a socket, a bulb, and two wires a child can make a light go on. It usually takes some time before the child makes all of the right connections. But once a child discovers that a light goes on when a circuit is completed, many more discoveries follow. The child tries to make two lights go on, or tries to make the lights brighter.

The materials involved are easy to find and easy to use. They are self-instructional. The child sees the results of his efforts quickly. A light either goes on or it does not. It either burns more brightly or it does not. Eventually, a child can try to wire a house board or even a small doll house.

Magnetism

There are many kinds of magnets and many shapes. Some look like bars, some like horseshoes, and some like thin paper which can be cut with a scissors. They all attract metals containing iron.

Children enjoy testing materials to see if objects are attracted by a magnet. They can try to discover how to make a magnet stronger. Is magnetic attraction stopped by a piece of paper? By some cardboard? By water? By a thin sheet of aluminum? By a sheet of iron? What happens when a magnet comes in contact with another magnet? With iron filings? With sugar? With a mixture of iron filings and sand?

Children quickly discover that objects can be sorted into "those that are attracted by a magnet" and "those that are not attracted by a magnet." They may even learn how to use a magnet to find a needle in a haystack.

Floating and Sinking

Soap A floats in water and soap B (about the same size) sinks. A cork floats but a piece of tile sinks. A piece of plasticine in the form of a ball sinks. The same piece of plasticine rolled out and shaped into a boat floats.

Almost any object in a classroom can be tested. Does it float? Does it sink? Is there a way to change objects that sink so that they can float? What can one do to objects that float in order to make them sink?

Because of the wide number of usable materials and the ease with which they can

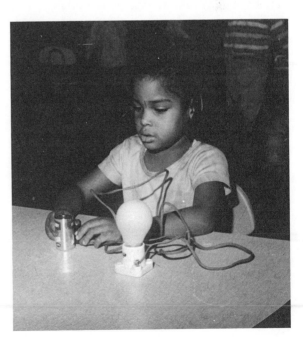

be handled, children enjoy this topic. It is rare for a child to be able to tell why an object floats or sinks. Yet many children can predict which objects in a set will float and which will sink.

Sound

Most children are aware that they hear many sounds around them almost all of the time. A bell may ring or a horn may honk. A jet may fly over their house or their classroom. A child may cry or squeal with joy.

Have they experienced the "feel" of a sound? Do they know how to make a sound louder or quieter? Can they change the pitch of a sound? How many different sounds can they hear while walking outside? Can they recognize the sound of their friend's voice when they hear it on a tape recording?

There are many materials available to help children answer some of these questions. The materials may be found in most classrooms. They can also be constructed by children. A jug band can be formed. A violin can be made from a cigar box, a stick, a few screws, and some wire. Soft drink bottles filled with different amounts of water make interesting sounds.

Nature provides some exciting sounds. Listen to the sounds of the leaves in a tree. Birds and insects make many kinds of sounds. Water rushing over rocks in a stream or the surf breaking on a shore are sounds worth hearing.

A child may discover that all sounds have something in common. They are made by objects that are vibrating (moving back and forth) rapidly. Other children may not make this discovery. Some learn to pay more attention to sounds, and to look for the source of the sounds. These are valuable skills for a child.

Living Things – Indoors

A child may learn a great deal about birth, life, and death without studying those specific topics. Much can be learned by observing a fish tank. New guppies are born.

Plants grow. Some plants die or are eaten by the fish. The water becomes murky at times. Fish die. The aquarium is constantly changing.

A child may desire his own small fish tank. Some sand, water, water plants, and two fish (a male and a female) can be used. A plastic one-gallon aquarium or a large glass jar may be used as the container.

Children can observe or care for small animals in a classroom. Gerbils or guinea pigs are commonly used. The animals grow and change in appearance. Sometimes they give birth and sometimes they die. Children learn more than facts about living. They learn to respect life.

Plants are living things that children can care for and raise, too. Using lima beans, a milk container, and some soil, children can learn about the conditions that help growth. They can also discover what happens when they over-water their plants. They can find out about the role of heat and light in plant growth. All of these things can be done without the direct help of adults.

Outdoor Activities

Some of the activities involving living things can be done out-of-doors as well as in the classroom. Some are even better when carried on outside the classroom. A garden can be planted and tended. Children can discover that seeds look different from one another. They can also find out that the things which grow from seeds look different, too.

Insects, birds (a bird feeder is a big help), and small rodents (mice and squirrels) can be observed by children. The children should be cautioned not to disturb the birds or animals. However, learning how to study these small animals from a distance is a valuable experience.

Children can understand their environment as part of an informal outdoor sciencing experience. They can learn about the weather and how to look for clues for predicting weather. They can look for examples of pollution. They can observe what happens to leaves in the fall and to rainwater in the spring. They can discover what happens to a snowman as the sun shines down and temperatures go up.

A Reminder

Informal sciencing is a child's activity. It is meant to be initiated and carried out

by children. It may be a daily activity or a weekly happening. Some children may not touch a simple set of materials. This is the way informal sciencing is meant to be carried out.

Teachers can help children. A reminder or a word of encouragement is helpful. A general rule for an adult who is supervising informal sciencing activities is: do not hover over the children. Of course, the children must be supervised so as not to endanger themselves or others, but they should be given enough freedom to learn what they want and to learn at their own rate. The materials, and the actions of the children, not the teachers, should produce the learning.

INCIDENTAL SCIENCING

A teacher tells the following story:

I was outside with my group of ten four-year-olds on a warm and humid spring morning. Suddenly one of the children looked up and to the west and shouted, "Look at that big black cloud!"

I looked up, along with most of the children and saw the darkest clouds I'd ever seen. The entire western sky looked black. The wind began to howl and the children became very excited.

"Gather all the toys and equipment and put them in the shed. Be quick!" I instructed.

We hurried indoors and rushed over to some windows that faced the west. The clouds were approaching at a fast speed. Trees began to bend under the force of the wind.

Lightning was flashing and the lights in the classroom blinked on and off.

"Move away from the windows," I urged the children.

Some children stood looking at the storm with amazement. Two of the children began to cry.

"Come over to the reading corner. I have a story I'd like to read to you. It's about a storm such as this." The children joined me and just as I started reading, the storm struck. There was a flash of lightning and then a huge crashing sound was heard. The rain fell, the lightning flashed, and the thunder crashed for about twenty minutes.

Then, almost as suddenly as it started, the rain stopped. The sky cleared and the sun came out. The class hurried to the windows. Rivers of water seemed to be everywhere. The huge maple tree — the one from which a tire swing hung — was completely uprooted. There was a great break in the ground where the roots had been. Never before had this group of children experienced a storm such as this, or seen a huge tree lying on the ground with its root system exposed. The children wanted to go outside to inspect the tree. They wanted to look at the roots.

How does a teacher deal with a situation such as this? It may be a once-in-a-lifetime opportunity. Does one ignore the children's excitement?

A teacher can use this opportunity to carry out an *incidental sciencing lesson.* A lesson such as this is almost always related to an incident that a number of children have experienced. In the case just described the children experienced a wind and rain storm.

The teacher, in this case, allowed the children to explore the tree. First she made certain that no electrical wires had been downed. She then allowed the children to explore the various parts of the tree using all of their senses.

After a period of time the teacher called the children together. She asked those who were interested to join her to discuss the storm and the tree. Those who were not interested were allowed to carry out another activity. She discussed what had happened. The children were asked to think about what they had observed. The teacher also asked them about their feelings. The darkness of the sky, the flashing lightning and the high winds were discussed.

The next day the village foresters came to the school. They showed the children some of the parts of the tree. Then they used chain saws to cut the tree apart. Children were able to see the growth rings of the tree. They observed the way in which the bark and the cork layer were attached.

The local television weatherman came to the school and spoke about storms. Only those children who were interested took part in these activities. Almost every child was interested.

THE MEANING OF INCIDENTAL SCIENCING

Over a period of time people experience a number of incidents as part of their life. Some incidents leave a lasting memory; others are quickly forgotten. Some are interesting to many people, and others interest only a few. Many of the incidents occur without warning, such as the sudden storm.

Things happen. An alert teacher will discover that children's curiosities have been aroused. At the proper moment the teacher can take advantage of the situation and carry out an incidental sciencing lesson.

It is not a carefully planned lesson. Materials are not always available. However, a discussion, an exploration, a demonstration, or a discovery about a topic can be started. It may last several minutes, or an hour. Children might ask questions for a month. Outside experts can later be involved.

Situations That Lead to Incidental Sciencing

An incidental sciencing lesson is not planned; it usually just happens. However,

an adult must be alert to the situations that lead to such a lesson.

- *Natural events.* Snowstorms, thunderstorms, volcanic eruptions, even a flock of migrating birds can capture the imaginations of children. Events such as these can often be used as the starting point for an incidental sciencing lesson.

- *Man-made events.* A moon landing, a ship launching, the construction of a

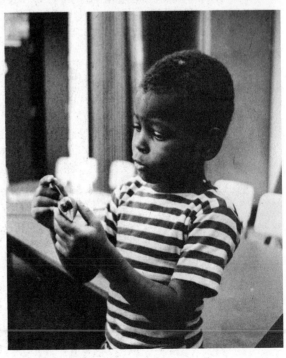

building (using bulldozers and other earth movers), the tearing down of a building are all examples of man-made events that can lead to interesting lessons.

- *Events related to the lives of the children.* A baby may be born into a child's family. A child or a child's relative may go into a hospital for surgery. These and other events related to a child's life can lead to worthwhile incidental sciencing lessons.

SUMMARY

In addition to formal sciencing, there are two other types of activities. These are informal sciencing and incidental sciencing.

Informal sciencing is a free investigation activity in which children select their own materials and do their own exploring. Teachers are encouraged to provide a setting and opportunities for children to work, but it is the children who decide whether to participate or not. A sciencing corner with needed materials and work space should be provided.

Incidental sciencing is built around incidents that take place in or around a school. The incidents are usually not planned. An alert teacher will take advantage of a situation as it occurs. Children are not forced to take part in the incidental sciencing activities. Natural events, man-made events, and events related to the lives of children are good starting points for incidental sciencing.

SUGGESTED ACTIVITIES

Obtain a science supply catalogue. Imagine that $50.00 can be spent on equipment to be used for formal sciencing.

- What electrical equipment should be bought?
- How many kinds of magnets can be bought? How much would be spent on magnets?
- What, if anything, would be purchased for floating and sinking?
- How much would be spent on sound-related materials? What would be purchased?
- How much would be spent on materials that help children learn about living things?

REVIEW

A.   Complete the following by choosing the best answer.

1. In informal sciencing the teacher's role is

   a. Of central importance.
   b. More important than that of children.
   c. To give little, if any, direct help.
   d. To control class behavior and carry out a review discussion.

2. Informal sciencing requires

   a. More teacher involvement than formal sciencing.
   b. Less teacher involvement than formal sciencing.
   c. No equipment.
   d. Less equipment than formal sciencing.

3. Two topics that could be included in informal sciencing are

    a. Sound and electricity.

    b. Sound and atomic structure.

    c. Molecules and electricity.

    d. Electricity and atomic structure.

4. In informal sciencing, children tend to

    a. Investigate in large groups.

    b. Read and look at pictures.

    c. Investigate on their own.

    d. Follow teacher directions only.

5. A basic goal of informal sciencing is to help children

    a. Feel successful.

    b. Learn basic science facts.

    c. Develop scientific approaches to research.

    d. Understand simple astronomy.

B.   Short Answer or Discussion

1. In selecting equipment and materials for informal sciencing a teacher should be concerned with six things. Name four of them.

2. List five topics that are appropriate for informal sciencing.

3. Describe two situations which a teacher can use as the starting point of an incidental sciencing lesson.

unit 5 the role of the teacher in planning sciencing activities

OBJECTIVES

At the end of this unit the reader should be able to

- State a definition of learning.
- List three steps a teacher should follow in preparing for a formal sciencing activity.
- Name and describe five sources for acquiring materials to be used in informal sciencing.

A good teacher does not just teach. This is because a teacher cannot force children to learn. Instead, a good teacher provides children with many opportunities to take part in a wide variety of activities. While the children take part, some of them learn facts. Some learn that they do not like the activities. Some find out that the activities are fun. Some can learn without the help of anyone else. All of these learning abilities are valuable.

A child may eagerly take part in activity A, but not like activity B at all. The same child may dislike activity C one day and like it a week later. It is very difficult to know in advance how every child will respond to each experience. They will respond, however.

Thus a teacher's concern is not just with teaching. The concentration must be on helping all children learn. When teachers understand that children learn what they experience, they will provide children with many experiences.

WHAT IS LEARNING?

There is a very simple definition of learning. It is helpful in planning learning experiences for children.

> Learning is exploring in order to discover personal meaning.

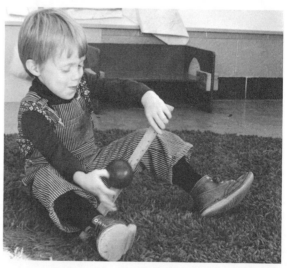

46

Exploring means that the children get directly involved. They become a part of their own experience. They are not only observers, they are participants. When participating, they move things around and mix things together. Children are not scolded for doing this, but rather are encouraged to explore.

The purpose of their explorations is to look for and find *personal meaning*. New experiences are added to those already had and there is an effort to make sense out of it all. When children are able to make some sense of their explorations, they have gained personal meaning.

Suppose a package arrives in the mail which, when opened, is found to contain a gold pen in a carrying case. It looks like a regular ball-point pen. However, as the carrying case is opened, the pen jumps out of the case and flies up to the ceiling of the room. How could this happen? What can be done to find out?

The ways in which one explores this situation determines what will be learned and how well it is learned. Does it conform to other experiences with ball-point pens? It looks, feels, and smells like an ordinary pen. However, when "dropped," it goes up to the ceiling, not down to the floor.

In order to learn from this situation one must gain some personal meaning from it. Maybe the pen has a special magnet in it. Perhaps it is all in your imagination. Both of these are ways of making personal sense out of a situation that does not make sense. Each possibility must be tried (explored). If neither explains your observation then more exploration is needed. The situation should be explored until some sense can be made of it. When a personal meaning has been given to the experience, then something is learned.

Children need to have a variety of experiences, and to make sense of those experiences. Therefore, if (1) a teacher's job is to help create opportunities for children to learn and (2) learning is the exploration and discovery of personal meaning, it follows that:

- A teacher must provide time for children to explore.

- A teacher must provide materials with which discoveries can be made.

- Teachers must create situations in which children make discoveries.

- Children must be allowed and encouraged to seek personal meanings to their discoveries.

PLANNING FORMAL SCIENCING EXPERIENCES

Good formal lessons and activities do not just happen. They are carefully planned. When dealing with formal sciencing, certain steps should be followed.

1. Decide the objectives of an activity. What are the children expected to achieve? What skills can the children acquire? What information? What sorts of attitudes?

2. Think of some of the ways children can become involved in a particular activity.

What can they do, given their age and their abilities? What builds and maintains the interests of children?

3. Gather and prepare materials that help children learn. What is available? Where can materials be found? How much do they cost? Are the materials safe for children to use?

4. Create the proper learning climate for the children. Are all needed materials available? Are they in working order? Are guidelines clear? Are children being encouraged (but not forced) to participate?

5. Study the outcomes of the learning activities. What have children learned? Was the learning pleasurable? What changes might be needed?

Figure 5-1 is a checklist to help teachers plan formal sciencing activities.

PLANNING INFORMAL SCIENCING EXPERIENCES

It is necessary to plan informal sciencing experiences as carefully as the formal ones. There is an important key to success in informal sciencing. A variety of attractive and

WHAT TO DO TO GET READY	YES	NO
Getting ready		
1. Have I read and do I understand the activities?	☐	☐
2. Have I gathered all the necessary materials?	☐	☐
3. Are tables and other work areas cleared and ready to be used?	☐	☐
Introducing activity		
1. Are materials out and within the children's reach?	☐	☐
2. Are children wearing proper clothing?	☐	☐
3. Has a motivating method been prepared?	☐	☐
Carrying out the activity		
1. Have I tried to anticipate questions children will ask?	☐	☐
2. Have I thought about the problems children might have?	☐	☐
3. Have I thought about ways to encourage children?	☐	☐
4. Have I considered what children can do who finish this activity quickly?	☐	☐
Evaluating the experience		
1. Do I know how to recognize whether a child has been successful in this activity?	☐	☐
2. Do I have some evaluative questions prepared for the children?	☐	☐

Fig. 5-1 A checklist for planning formal sciencing activities.

usable materials must be available to the children. And, of course, children must feel free to participate in informal sciencing activities.

Gathering Materials

A key to successful informal sciencing is in the type and amount of materials available to the children. It is the job of the teacher to gather and package the materials. Thus, one must know what materials to look for and where to look. A good way to begin is to decide on the topics to be used in the informal phase. In unit 4 of this text six topics are suggested. There are others that can be used, too. Almost any science-related topic is appropriate for informal sciencing if:

- A child can safely participate in activities without close teacher supervision.

- A child can carry out investigations of his own choosing without close teacher direction.

Once the topics are decided upon, a list of materials should be drawn up. This list can be determined in a number of ways:

- Personal experience can help one in deciding which materials are needed.

- A science supply catalogue can provide ideas and information about materials related to certain science topics.

- A science methods text or a science activity book can suggest materials.

- Common sense can help one decide on certain materials that are valuable in selected activities.

After the list of needed materials is made up, it is necessary to find the equipment. Here are a few suggestions:

- Many items can be purchased from science equipment suppliers. Each supplier prints a catalogue with pictures and descriptions of materials. However, these materials tend to be more expensive than items purchased locally.

- Materials and equipment can be found in discount stores, catalogue stores and local variety stores.

- Many items can be purchased at wholesale stores, rummage sales, and auctions.

- Local schools sometimes sell oversupplies of materials or discard equipment that can be restored to use. Occasionally, schools close and sell all of their equipment at very reasonable prices.

- Local industries may sell at small cost or give away materials that are useful for informal sciencing. Many items discarded by manufacturers as waste can be reclaimed and used.

- Department stores and other retail stores are a good local source of supplies and equipment.

- Parents may be willing to loan, donate, or purchase needed materials.

- Local organizations can be asked to collect money or materials for a school's sciencing program.

Regardless of the source, equipment should be well constructed and sturdy. It must be appropriate for young children to handle. It cannot be too small. It should not be so large that youngsters cannot handle it.

Arranging Materials

After the equipment has been gathered it should be stored in a way that children can use it easily. The materials should be easy to reach and easy to identify. Things that go together should be stored together. Children should be told that certain pieces of equipment go together. One way of doing this is to place materials that relate to a given topic in a color-coded container. For example, all equipment used to study sound can be placed in a red cardboard box. A shoe box can also be painted (use semi-gloss or glossy enamel paint since latex base paints run when exposed to water) and used for storage. Any sturdy cardboard, plastic, or wooden container can be used. It is useful to remember these things about storage:

- Place all of the informal sciencing materials in the same general location in a room. A corner set of shelves or a special closet can be used.

- Materials should be low enough on shelves so that children can easily and safely reach them.

- Use small containers. Heavy boxes can be dangerous and a dropped box can cause much damage.

- Arrange materials so they appear attractive to the children. Ripped containers should be replaced. Broken materials should be thrown away.

- Use a color-coding system or some other scheme for identifying materials. Individual items that do not fit into containers should also be color-coded in some way. A child should know that all equipment and materials related to a

given topic have the same color-coding. This is helpful both in selecting materials and in returning them to the shelf for storage.

PLANNING FOR INCIDENTAL SCIENCING

As was pointed out in an earlier unit incidental sciencing is not highly organized or well planned. It usually just happens. An injured bird may be found. The children become interested in blood. They want to know what it is. Where does it come from? Do all animals have blood? Is blood always red?

If a house or building near the school is being torn down, children can observe the process and may become interested. They ask about the names of the machines that are being used. How do the large machines work? Why does the building have such large wooden beams? What happens to the scrap materials after the building is torn down?

Alert and curious children have many questions about the world around them. A teacher or parent can discourage this interest or encourage the child. It all depends on the reaction of the adult when the child asks a question or states an interest.

A child may hear answers to his questions that sound like this:

I don't have time for that now.

That isn't important.

You will learn about that when you get older.

You're supposed to be finger painting.

You ask too many questions.

On the other hand, an adult can answer children's questions in this way:

That is a good question. Let's get together and see what we can do to figure out the answer.

Would you like to try to find some answers on your own? If not, perhaps I can help you.

What do *you* think about it?

Is anyone interested in. . .? I'll be happy to have a little sciencing discussion with those who are.

I'm very pleased that you make such good observations. Would you like to share your questions with other people?

What Can a Teacher Do?

In incidental sciencing the only planning a teacher can do is to be alert. One can be alert to current events. For instance, if an eclipse of the sun is about to happen, many questions from the children can be expected.

If a space shuttle experiment is about to take place, many children may show interest in this. If a snowstorm or a hurricane is predicted, children will want information.

A teacher can also be alert to the day-to-day happenings in and around the school. The birth of guinea pigs, the death of a gold fish, or the falling of leaves may excite some children. They will want to know more about these events. Their interests should be met.

In addition to being alert to events, a teacher can prepare for incidental sciencing by reading about current events. A good teacher should try to understand some of the basic areas that excite children. These include questions about: birth, death, space, the moon, unidentified flying objects (UFO's), dinosaurs, monsters, stormy weather, and flight (birds and airplanes). One can prepare for questions and events by reading about those things.

This does not mean that the teacher can be ready for every question, but one can be better prepared. Above all, one can be alert to the moment when a child shows interest, and encourage questions.

It must be remembered, however, that incidental sciencing starts with the children. They should show interest. They should ask questions. Then the effective teacher takes over and stimulates learning and understanding.

SUMMARY

The key to whatever good and bad things happen to children in a classroom is the teacher and how that role is perceived. The notion that teachers teach information and learners receive that information should be rejected. Learning is the exploration and discovery of personal meaning. Thus children must be given the time and opportunity to explore and work out a personal meaning from experiences.

Much teacher planning and preparation goes into formal sciencing. It is the children, however, who do the work and discover meaning in both process and content areas.

Teacher involvement takes place in the planning for informal sciencing, too. The teacher must decide on topics, list and gather materials, and prepare a work area for the children. The teacher must also prepare a classroom climate that encourages children to participate in informal sciencing activities.

There is somewhat less preparation by a teacher for incidental sciencing. In order to recognize the proper time for incidental sciencing a teacher must learn to be alert. A teacher can also prepare by knowing some broad, general information about topics of interest to children.

SUGGESTED ACTIVITIES

- Ask ten experienced teachers to define the following terms:

  teacher
  learner
  teaching
  learning

  a. How many teachers consider their role to be the active one and the learner's role to be the passive one?

  b. How many teachers indicate that the responsibility for learning is in the hands of the learner?

c. How do you think the role of a teacher should be defined?

- Develop a teacher checklist that could be used for planning an informal sciencing program.

- Obtain a science equipment catalogue. Page through the catalogue and identify equipment that could be purchased in each of the following areas:

electricity
magnetism
sound

- Answer the following questions:

  a. How much would you have to spend in order to buy small quantities (not more than five of each) of these materials for an informal sciencing program?

  b. For as many as possible try to think up less expensive materials that might do the same job. How much would the less expensive materials cost?

- Go to a library or bookstore and make a list of information sources (texts, easy reading books, magazines) in the following topic areas:

Weather
The seasons
Space and rockets
The human body

Think of the ways in which everyday experiences with children might lead to discussions in each of the areas.

REVIEW

1. Write a definition of learning.
2. List four sources of materials for informal sciencing.
3. How can one determine whether a topic is appropriate for informal sciencing?
4. State two ways a teacher can prepare for incidental sciencing.

unit 6 the role of the teacher in implementing sciencing activities

OBJECTIVES

At the end of this unit the reader should be able to

- List three suggestions for helping children succeed in formal sciencing.
- Name and describe four instructional procedures that add to the variety of the formal sciencing program.
- Describe two ways in which children's misunderstandings can be cleared up.
- List the six commandments for teachers.

Formal sciencing is that portion of the total sciencing program in which the teacher plays the most vital role. It is relatively easy for a teacher to let children "play around" with materials in the informal phase of sciencing. But in the formal phase of the program the teacher plays a more active and central role. Because of this active involvement it is also easier for a teacher to let the role become too central. The teacher can easily dominate the entire program — and in the process ruin every activity. With this in mind, a number of suggestions are provided for the teacher in this unit. In addition, a number of teaching techniques are described.

STARTING THE LESSON

After planning and understanding the objectives and directions for each activity; after gathering all of the materials needed to carry out an activity; and after arranging the classroom so that the activity can be carried out, then the activity can be begun.

An important part of any lesson is the way it is started. This is true of a formal sciencing lesson, too. Children's attentions need to be "grabbed." They need to be motivated to the activity and their attentions directed to the key elements in the lesson.

A *grabber activity* may consist of a small explosion. It may be a flash of light or the sound of instruments being played. Another example of a grabber activity is shown in the following story on page 55.

A teacher is about to carry out an activity designed to demonstrate to the children that objects can be identified by the odor they give off. The class has been playing out-of-doors. While they were outside a parent helper went back into the classroom and got out a popcorn popper, some oil, and some popcorn. She placed the popper in a corner of the room, behind some large cartons. She then added the oil and popcorn and plugged the electric popper into the electrical outlet.

As the children returned from outside each one entered the room and sniffed.

"Popcorn! We smell popcorn!" shouted the children.

"What makes you think it's popcorn?" asked the teacher.

"I know what popcorn smells like," insisted one child. "That's the smell of popcorn."

"My mother makes popcorn for me sometimes," called another. "I'd know that smell anywhere."

"But where's the smell coming from?" asked the teacher.

The children began sniffing about the room. "It's strongest in the corner," said one of the girls.

The popcorn started to pop, making quite a loud noise.

"It is popcorn for sure! I hear it popping!" insisted the children.

At last the teacher confirmed what all the children already knew. Popcorn was indeed being prepared in the classroom. The teacher pursued the question of how the children knew they had been smelling popcorn. They finally decided that from past experience they knew what the smell of popcorn was like. They also agreed that they could recognize many things by the smell given off. Several children even suggested that they could be blindfolded and they would identify substances using the sense of smell.

The children were excited and were mentally prepared to begin the lesson. They felt a challenge. How many items could they identify by smell alone? Could they learn to recognize some new substances by smell alone?

It can be seen from the preceding situation that a grabber activity does not have to be long and involved. It does not require a laboratory full of equipment. It needs only to attract the children's interests and to direct them toward an activity.

INCREASING A CHILD'S SUCCESS

One of the most important objectives of sciencing is to help children see themselves as

able performers to help them develop a positive self-image. A good way for a positive self-concept to develop is for a child to experience success. The child must know that he has been successful, and that others recognize his success.

There are no absolute ways a teacher can guarantee that a child will be successful. However, there are some things a teacher can do to increase the likelihood of a child's success. They are:

- *Avoid too much talking.* Young children learn from their own experiences, not by being told about their teacher's experiences. Too much talk, especially at the start of an activity, disturbs many children. They are anxious to get started. Sciencing is doing. It is an activity for children.

- *Provide children with plenty of materials.* There should be a large number and a large variety of materials and equipment. In formal sciencing the ideal arrangement is for each child to have a set of materials. All sets should be alike.

- *Make certain that materials are attractive and safe.* Before beginning an activity all materials should be checked over. Everything necessary should be there and be in working order. Children should be attracted to the materials. Soiled, foul smelling, torn, and damaged things tend to repel children.

- *Avoid being overly helpful — hovering is not helpful.* Many teachers want to be helpful. They don't want children to become frustrated. Therefore, they peek over children's shoulders. When a child puts two objects together incorrectly the teacher takes the objects and puts the things together the way they are supposed to go. Then the objects are returned to the child and the child is told to continue the investigation.

When this happens, children learn that they are not going to *really* be allowed to investigate. They are forced to do what the teacher wants in the way the teacher wants it to be done. Children quickly learn that they aren't investigating and experimenting. They are conforming. This is not the intent of sciencing. Hovering over children is not helpful. Children should be allowed to learn from their errors.

- *Allow for individual differences.* Given the same kinds of materials and the same

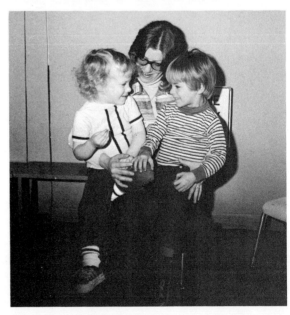

general instructions three children may attack the same problem in three different ways. And they may all solve the problem using their own approach. Moreover, some interesting things may happen when children solve problems using their own approach. They may uncover a new problem that is more interesting than the one they started on. Perhaps they will make a totally unexpected discovery, or develop a skill that had not been planned for in the teacher's activity guide.

Children need the opportunity to express their individuality. Given a set of materials and some general idea of what the materials can be used for, several things can happen:

a. A child may ask at the beginning for specific directions. What should step one be? Then what is step two and step three? This child needs teacher guidance and teacher attention.

b. A child may begin working with materials but after a few minutes need direction. A hint may be enough to get the child going again.

c. A child may "dive into" the materials and work for as long as thirty minutes without the need of adult attention.

d. A child may refuse to participate. Experience has shown that it is useless to force a child to take part. It is better to let this child do other productive things. If a particular activity is well planned, most children will gladly take part. The nonparticipant will usually return to the activity if other children continue to work on it. The child does not want to miss out on all the fun.

- *Provide an atmosphere of freedom.* Children should feel that they have options in an activity. In order to investigate and discover, children need to feel free. It is the job of a teacher to create the feeling of freedom for children. Once this feeling is created, children will risk being inquisitive experimenters. They are not afraid to try something new and different. They will find that they can learn from their errors. It is only in an atmosphere such as this that children can benefit from sciencing activities. In this atmosphere, children are more likely to develop positive self-images and to learn and develop skills.

TYPES OF INSTRUCTIONAL PROCEDURES

There is more than one way for children to learn an idea or develop a skill. A position taken in this text is that all children need to feel successful. A feeling of success comes from performing well in school-like activities. Various children perform best in a variety of learning situations. As described in the previous section some children need much direction and some need little. Some children learn best when watching a television program. Some learn best when learning in a group. Others learn best when working alone. No one activity or approach can be expected to meet the needs of all children.

Children's interests, experiences, backgrounds, and upbringing are varied. Therefore, activities designed for children must be varied. There are several types of instructional procedures that are suggested for formal sciencing. Each procedure is designed to provide variety in the program. In that way each child at some time will have a chance to use a procedure designed to bring out what that child can do best.

Telling things. Various verbal techniques can be used for certain purposes. See figure 6-1.

Instructional media. There is a wide variety of media and materials that can be used for instructional purposes in sciencing. See figure 6-2.

Demonstrations. There are times when a teacher may wish to perform a demonstration for the class. In a demonstration lesson the teacher manipulates equipment and the children observe the results. Small numbers of children can be involved in a demonstration as helpers or describers. See figure 6-3.

Guided learning. Some activities require more direction and explanation than others. Therefore, it is sometimes useful to provide directions to a group of children in such a way that they are led to make a discovery. This technique is widely used. However, teachers must be careful not to dominate the activity to the point where children stop working. See figure 6-4.

Open learning. In open learning (or free discovery) children work on their own. They follow their own interests. They seek their own answers. Only through the materials provided for them are the children guided. Of the instructional procedures that can be used in formal sciencing, this is the most highly recommended one.

Technique	Use
Direct telling	1. Motivating children by telling a story 2. Explaining directions 3. Clarifying possible dangers 4. Providing needed background information (this should not be a long lecture)
Discussions	1. Teacher with individual children to provide (explain) information or evaluate progress 2. Teacher with small groups of children to clarify learning 3. Teacher with the entire group to end an activity 4. Children with other children to clarify findings, compare results, resolve differences

Fig. 6-1 Verbal techniques

Type of media	Use
Television and radio	1. To motivate and to demonstrate 2. To look for examples such as variety of sounds and colors; changes 3. To provide information not directly available to children
Slides, filmstrips, and motion pictures	1. To motivate 2. To show examples 3. To provide new information not directly available to children
Tape recordings and records	1. To motivate 2. To help in the learning/discovery process such as recording sounds; listening to sounds of musical instruments

Fig. 6-2 Types of media

Type of demonstration	Purpose
To explain a concept or show an example	Some equipment is dangerous to use or expensive. It would not be in the children's best interests to handle this equipment. For example: to show how colors change under black light (using fluorescent chalk or crayons); to show that mixing baking soda and vinegar results in the production of a colorless gas that puts out flame.
To show how to use equipment	To demonstrate how to build a simple aquarium to study change; to show how to pour liquid from one glass to another, etc.

Fig. 6-3 Types of demonstrations

Example	Purpose
The children are given three cups of water. One is very warm, a second is room temperature, and the third is very cold. The children are then guided through simple directions by the teacher to place an ice cube in each cup. The children observe the changes in size and shape of the ice cubes. Using a large thermometer the children can compare changes and relate them to the water in the cups. The teacher guides the children to discover that the greatest change takes place in the cup of hot water.	1. To discover a new piece of information 2. To discover a way of investigating; learning a skill
Use of games is a form of guided learning. The children are given materials and learn a concept or skill as a result of playing the game. For example, a bingo game involving recognition of colors can be created. Colors are named and the children cover squares of that color.	1. Children can discover new information 2. Children can learn an investigative skill
The children can be led to extend learnings they have already made. Guided learning involving teacher directions, suggestions, or hints can lead to follow-up discoveries. For example, a child has discovered that ice changes rapidly in size and shape in hot water. The teacher can suggest using water of various temperatures and food coloring. Children are guided to drop food coloring into the water and observe the results. Where did changes occur the fastest?	1. To guide children in a way that they feel encouraged to extend a series of observations 2. To provide clues to using new materials or to making additional discoveries 3. To help children relate experiences in one activity to findings in another

Fig. 6-4 Guided learning techniques

- Example: Children are given the following materials: red, blue, yellow, and white tempera paints; water; several stirrers; and ten baby food jars. The only directions they receive are: "See how many colors can be created by using the powders and the water. If more baby food jars are needed they are available. When satisfied with the colors created, paint a picture using the newly created colors."

At this point, the teacher steps back and permits children to experiment with the colors. The teacher is free to move about the room, and talk to individual children. After a period of time, a few children may become tired of this activity. The teacher can then discuss with them what they observed as they mixed the paints. They can name the colors created. They can be asked to describe the differences between the tempera powders and the final liquid products. The teacher can ask what the white does to other colors.

As other children complete the activity they, too, can be given a chance to discuss their findings. The key objectives in an activity such as this involve: a) learning about and observing change; b) learning about solids and liquids; c) identifying colors by name;

d) relating variations in color to a basic color (pink is a form of red); e) classifying colors; and f) investigating (much as a scientist would) to discover the answers to problems.

All of these objectives can and should be achieved with little help from a teacher. This is the purpose of open learning.

GENERAL CONSIDERATIONS

There a number of questions teachers ask about implementing formal sciencing lessons. They want to know how to respond to certain questions put forth by children. They are interested in ways of clearing up false information that is sometimes brought out in the course of discovery. How does one determine whether an activity has been successful? Each of these topics is discussed in the paragraphs following.

Answering Children's Questions

Should all questions be answered? Which ones should and which should not?

All questions do not require answers. In fact, attempting to answer some questions presents more problems than it solves. In particular, questions of causality (why does the sun shine? Why does the rain fall from the clouds?) create serious problems for teachers and children alike. The correct answers to many such questions are so complicated that to try to answer them causes great confusion. For example, three- to five-year-olds are not prepared to deal with the concept of gravity. Yet it is not possible to explain why rain falls to earth without explaining gravitational forces.

Efforts should be made to change questions about why things happen to observational questions. What happened? Tell what happened in detail. In what order did things happen? Questions like these are within the mental capabilities of young children. They can generate their own answers to questions like these.

Children also ask many procedural questions. How do I do this? Where can I find materials? Questions of this type may or may not be answered immediately. If a child needs to know where equipment is stored the answer should be given immediately and accurately. If, however, a child prefers not to think through a problem (Tell me what to do!), it may be necessary to delay the answer for a while. It is possible to respond to children's questions without giving a direct answer. For instance:

Child: "What should I do?"

Teacher: "What have you done so far?" or

"What might you do with this piece of equipment?" or

"Tell me what *you* think you might do." or

"Is there an answer to your question? Might there be many things you could do?"

In some cases children ask questions but aren't really interested in the answers. They are seeking adult attention. They hope to avoid uncomfortable, problem solving situations. A teacher must use good judgment in answering questions. The temptation to tell the answer quickly should be avoided. Quick answers are sometimes misunderstood by children. Of even greater importance is the fact that quick answers cheat children of discovering for themselves.

A rule-of-thumb for formal sciencing is: Answer questions directly only if a child cannot get the answer for himself. Procedural questions should be answered if they are important.

CLARIFYING MISUNDERSTANDINGS

Whenever children are allowed to investigate and discover for themselves, some risk is involved. They may discover inaccurate answers. Their procedure may lead them to developing false notions. What should be done?

Clearly, false information should not go uncontested. False understandings can last a long time in a child's mind. It is very difficult to unlearn false information. The truth should be made clear as soon as possible. Three things can be done when a teacher recognizes that a child has learned some misinformation:

- The teacher can suggest that the child review his own findings and evidence. The child might be encouraged to do part of an investigation over. The child can then compare the new results to those first developed. For example, a child might report that he mixed red paint with blue paint and got a green color as a result. A teacher can suggest that the child get a clean container and mix the red and blue again. Then after a few minutes the teacher checks back with the child for results. If this time the child reports that the mixture resulted in a purple color the teacher and the child can discuss the next step.

Which is correct? Red + Blue = Green or
                                  Red + Blue = Purple

The child might be encouraged to look for additional ways of producing and confirming results.

- A child can be encouraged to check his findings with those of several other children in the group. The child can also discuss his procedures with other children. They can compare what they did as well as what they discovered. Sometimes it is helpful for a child to conduct an investigation with a group of children looking on. The child can carry out procedures with two or three helpers as assistants. The assistants may discover a procedural error.

- A child may refuse to acknowledge that his results are in error. It is then that the teacher should tell the child what went wrong. This should be done without insulting a child. For example, "That is a very interesting finding. I had always thought that five marbles is more than three marbles. Would you show me what you've done? Perhaps I can help you."

Children should be provided with "face-saving" devices when they produce inaccurate information. However, their inaccuracies should not go unchallenged.

EVALUATING SUCCESS

Has an activity been successful? Are changes in procedure called for? Have the children learned anything? These are questions many teachers ask. The answers are not easy to provide.

First, one must decide what is most important in an activity. What makes an activity successful or unsuccessful?

Some people say that activities are successful if 77 percent of the children achieve 59 percent of the objectives; or if 93 percent of the children achieve 82 percent of the objectives. Others insist that activities are successful if the children all had fun. If they enjoy an activity, it is a good activity. If they do not, it is a bad activity.

Both of these positions are extreme and should be avoided. Activities should provide children with a chance to learn. They should learn information. They should learn skills. They should develop attitudes. If a child learns information but does not enjoy learning, the quality of the activity may be to blame. If a child learns no skills or information but finds the activity very pleasant, this is better but also far from ideal.

Things to look for:	Yes	No
a. Did children participate willingly?	☐	☐
b. Did children use materials as expected?	☐	☐
c. Were children able to complete activities?	☐	☐
d. Did children tend to achieve knowledge objectives?	☐	☐
e. Were skill goals achieved?	☐	☐
f. Did children seem happy in their work?	☐	☐
g. Would you use this activity again?	☐	☐
h. What could be done to improve this activity?		

Fig. 6-5 A checklist for evaluating sciencing activities.

In evaluating the quality of sciencing activities, an informal checklist, such as that in figure 6-5, can be used. However, one must be cautious in using a simple checklist such as this. It is meant only to suggest some things to look for. A teacher's common sense and awareness of children is a better guide than any checklist.

If a checklist such as this is used, it should be completed by the teacher soon after the end of an activity. Children should not be aware that it is being used.

It is important to remember that formal evaluation of individual children is not recommended. Sciencing is meant to be a way for children to learn and to have fun in the process. It is geared toward putting children in situations that produce a feeling of success. For some children, an attempt to evaluate their achievements would make them uneasy. It might ruin the sciencing experience for them.

PARTICIPATION IN INFORMAL SCIENCING

The key to success in informal sciencing has to do with child participation. Equipment and materials can be made available to children. However, children cannot be forced to learn from their experiences. They can't be forced to enjoy what they are doing.

They can be encouraged to participate, to learn, and to gain pleasure from their experiences. It is the role of the supervising adult to provide the climate for children to learn. In informal sciencing a few simple suggestions can make a great deal of difference:

• Free choice periods should be provided for children each day. During these periods, the children should feel free to participate in any of a variety of activities. One of these activities is, of course, informal sciencing.

• When a child loses interest in a particular activity, the teacher can remind the child about informal sciencing. Sometimes a child needs to be reminded about the available electrical equipment or the magnets or the sound materials.

- One sometimes encounters a child who refuses to sit with the group for "story time." A child should not be forced to sit and listen to a story. The child can be encouraged, however, to try other productive activities. Informal sciencing is one of those activities.

- It is important that children do not feel forced into informal sciencing. They should think of it as a free choice activity.

GETTING CHILDREN STARTED

A group of ten children have been busy for ten minutes creating watercolor pictures. Suddenly, one of the children throws his paint brush on the floor. He then turns to his teacher and says that he does not feel like painting any more.

"What can I do now?" the child asks. "Clean up your paint materials and then we'll discuss some things you might try," replies the teacher.

After cleaning his brush and his cups of paint he returns to his teacher.

"Have you ever tried working in the free sciencing corner?" asks the teacher. "No," replies the child.

They walk over to the free (informal) sciencing corner. There are some low wooden bookshelves and a worktable in the corner. On the shelves are about a dozen shoe boxes. Some are painted red, some blue, green, yellow, or orange.

"If you look in these red boxes you will find objects that are part of a topic called magnetism," the teacher explains. "Feel free to work with these materials to see what you can find out. The only rule to follow when using these things is that, when finished, you return them to the same box they came from. Otherwise, feel free to investigate. See what you can find out about magnetism. Or, if magnetism does not interest you, you can work on a different topic. The orange boxes have electrical equipment in them. Yellow boxes contain materials related to sound. In the green boxes are materials for studying floating and sinking. The blue boxes have some equipment and materials for growing seeds. If any of the topics interest you, feel free to work on them. I will be available to help, but I will not answer all of your questions. Try to learn how to use the materials and find your own answers."

The teacher walks away to another part of the room but keeps an eye on the child. The child takes a yellow box and opens it up. He pokes around for a minute or two looking at the materials in the box. He then closes the cover and replaces it on the shelf. Next, he takes an orange box, places it on the worktable and takes out all of the materials. Carefully he inspects each item. He squeezes, pushes, rubs, and smells various things. Finally, he selects a bulb and a wire and looks around the classroom to find the teacher.

"What should I do with these? he asks.

"What do you think you might do with them?" replies the teacher.

The teacher may want to tell the child how to use a battery, bulb, and wires to create a circuit. However, the child may be developing a thought or an answer. Forcing the child to make a quick response or asking another question keeps the child from developing his own thoughts.

After a short time, the child says, "I think I should make the bulb light up."

"You have all the things you need to make that happen in the box where you found the bulb," the teacher replies.

The child returns to the table and tries several ways to connect wires to the bulb. He is not successful. The teacher should not rush to his aid. If the child is really interested, he will struggle with this problem. If he leaves it for today, he may return to it tomorrow. The teacher can tell the child that other materials in the box are needed to make the light glow. Perhaps the child will recognize that the battery is a needed part of the circuit. Through trial and error, and some frustration, the child finally gets the light to

glow. When the light goes on for the first time, the child feels a sense of accomplishment. He solved the problem by his own methods. This may have shown the child that he has valuable mental powers, or that he is a valuable person.

Much can be learned about the role of a teacher in informal sciencing from this preceding description. Note that:

- The teacher provided only minimum directions for the child. The directions were given in a casual and nonthreatening way. The child did not feel forced into doing anything.

- The teacher avoided answering the child's questions directly. Some of the child's questions were met with questions from the teacher: "What do you think?" and "How could you find out?"

- The teacher knew the materials that were available, and the learning that could take place. The child was provided with encouragement and helpful hints.

- The teacher did not volunteer information to the child. The child was encouraged to find answers to his own question. However, the teacher did watch for signs of frustration. Had the child become upset by the trial and error approach, help would be available.

- The teacher was aware of possible dangers to the child's health and safety. Precautions were taken so the child would not try to insert wires into the wall socket. A caution at the start can prevent hazards.

- The teacher made no effort to carry out a formal evaluation. A casual "tell me what you have done" is all the evaluation that was needed.

SIX COMMANDMENTS FOR THE TEACHER

In many ways the teacher's role both in formal and informal sciencing can best be summarized by these six "commandments."

1. Plan activities in ways that provide the largest number of children with maximum opportunities to discover concepts and relationships for themselves. This can best be accomplished when children have materials of their own with which to work, and enough freedom and time to carry out their investigations.

2. Accept the principle that no concept, relationship, or skill is so important that a child is made to feel that he has failed if he has been unable to understand or perform it.

3. Plan and carry out activities that allow children to learn investigative process skills as well as some simple concepts or facts.

4. If, in teaching a lesson or activity, insufficient materials are available to directly involve children in their own

learning, do not teach the lesson or begin the activity.

5. Do not talk too much. It is the child for whom the learning is intended. Too much teacher talk results in unmotivated and uninvolved children.

6. Do not force children to participate in either formal or informal sciencing. It is better to have children miss out on the potential gains than to create a strong negative feeling in them by forcing them to participate.

SUMMARY

Formal sciencing requires teacher attention both in the planning stage and when the activities are carried out. Children need to be motivated. They must be helped to succeed. This can be done by: avoiding too much talking; providing children with plenty of

materials; insuring that materials are attractive and safe to use; avoiding being overly helpful; allowing for individual differences; and providing an atmosphere of freedom. There are a number of instructional procedures that also help children succeed. They include: telling things; use of instructional media; demonstrations; guided learning; and open learning. No one type of activity or approach can be expected to meet the needs of all children. Therefore, each of the techniques should be used at one time or another.

Answering children's questions can be a problem in sciencing. Direct answers should be provided only if a child has tried but cannot find the answer alone. Misinformation that children may learn should be cleared up. However, children should not be made to feel inferior or stupid for coming up with wrong answers. Evaluation should be limited. Only informal approaches in which individual children are not involved should be used.

Informal sciencing differs from formal sciencing because informal sciencing is a free time activity. Children may or may not want to take part. Teachers do not force children into becoming involved. Few or no directions are given to children. The teacher's primary job is to provide encouragement to the child and a chance to work.

Circle the numeral that best describes the person you are observing	All of the time		Some of the time		Never
Teacher does the talking.	5	4	3	2	1
Teacher answers questions immediately and in detail.	5	4	3	2	1
Teacher is well-prepared; knows what to do.	5	4	3	2	1
Teacher provides child with information.	5	4	3	2	1
Teacher shows concern for children's safety.	5	4	3	2	1
Teacher evaluates learning very carefully and thoroughly.	5	4	3	2	1

Fig. 6-6 A checklist for observing a teacher.

SUGGESTED ACTIVITIES

- Using the checklist in figure 6-6, observe a teacher, teacher-aide or student teacher working with children for a period of ten minutes.

- Using the basic notion that some materials are solid and some are liquid do the following:

  a. Develop a plan for an activity using instructional media to help children identify solids.

  b. Develop a plan for an activity using a demonstration to help children identify liquids.

  c. Using a guided learning approach develop a plan for an activity that would help children tell the difference between a solid and a liquid.

  d. If possible, compare your plans with those of three other people. Exchange ideas and evaluate all of the plans.

  e. Use one of the plans with a small group of children.

- Work with a group of children for one hour without directly answering a question posed by a child. Try to guide children in answering their own questions. Have someone observe you and write down:

  a. How many questions were asked by the children?

  b. How many were answered?

  c. What did a child do when a question was not directly answered?

REVIEW

A.   Complete the following by choosing the best answer.

1. In formal sciencing, if the teacher dominates each activity, then
   a. Children learn more.
   b. Each activity is likely to be ruined.
   c. Teachers have more fun.
   d. Children develop a love for sciencing.

2. A teacher can help increase children's success in sciencing by
   a. Avoiding too much talk.
   b. Providing plenty of materials.
   c. Making certain that materials are safe.
   d. Doing all of the above.

3. To provide for individual differences, a teacher should
   a. Have all children doing the same thing at the same time.
   b. Give a child time and freedom to explore.
   c. Begin each activity with a discussion of "do's" and "don'ts."
   d. Force every child to participate.

4. In sciencing, a teaching strategy that can be followed is

    a. Direct telling.
    b. Use of instructional media, such as tape recorders.
    c. Demonstrations.
    d. All of the types listed in a, b, and c.

5. In open-learning type activities

    a. Teachers tell children what to discover.
    b. Teachers use tape-recorded instructions to tell children what to learn.
    c. Children work on their own.
    d. Children do not use materials.

6. The best way to evaluate children in sciencing is

    a. By means of a paper and pencil test.
    b. By means of an oral quiz.
    c. By observing their actions as they discuss activities.
    d. By using a checklist.

B.   Short Answer or Discussion

1. How does a teacher's role differ in informal sciencing from formal sciencing?

2. State the six commandments for teachers.

unit 7 the benefits of sciencing for the child, teacher, and school program

OBJECTIVES

At the end of this unit the reader should be able to

- State five ways in which a child can benefit from participating in sciencing activities.
- Describe two ways a teacher can benefit from sciencing.
- State one way a total school program can be improved through the use of sciencing activities.

This unit is designed to help the reader recognize the various benefits that are possible when children experience sciencing activities. Benefits for the teacher and the total program are described. A few drawbacks related to sciencing are also mentioned.

BENEFITS FOR THE CHILD

If teachers understand what sciencing is meant to do for children and how to plan, organize, and carry out activities, children will benefit in a number of ways. Some of the most basic prereading skills needed by a child can be developed in sciencing. In sciencing a child works directly with materials. Parts are fitted together. Objects are compared and changes observed in those objects. The child begins to develop *visual discrimination skills*, *auditory discrimination skills*, and *hand-eye skills.* In addition, the child develops concepts and learns words that can be used as he begins to read.

Visual discrimination. This involves the ability to use one's eyes to recognize differences in the way objects appear. For example, in figure 7-1, is A different from B? If so, how? In figure 7-2, which line is longer, C or D? (Use only your eyes to determine the answer.) In what ways are E, F, and G in figure 7-3 alike? Can at least six similarities be found? In what ways are they different?

Fig. 7-1. Are A and B exactly the same?

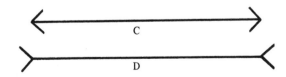

Fig. 7-2. Are lines C and D equal in length?

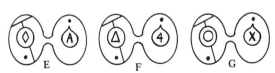

Fig. 7-3. What are the similar features of E, F, and G? How are they different?

To answer these questions one must be able to make visual discriminations. This is an especially important skill for children to have.

In order for a child to read, that child must be able to visually identify differences in letters. How does a P differ from R? How is O different from Q? If a child cannot recognize differences in letters the child will have problems with reading.

Experience has shown that through practice children can develop the ability to see very small differences in objects. They learn to look for ways in which objects are alike and different. They even learn to do it without being told to do it. It can be said that children develop a *mental set* (a tendency or willingness) for this skill.

But how do children develop this ability? They do it by having experiences with objects that are alike in some ways and different in others. They touch these objects. They smell them. And after many chances to work with these objects they begin to understand that things can be alike and they can be different. They begin to search out these likenesses and differences every chance they get. And once this begins to happen, the child can develop the skill called visual discrimination. The child has also increased the likelihood for success in reading.

Auditory discrimination. This is another skill that is very important to the young child. It involves the ability to hear likenesses and differences in sounds.

It may involve recognizing the difference between the sound of two instruments, such as a tuba and a trumpet. It may involve the ability to identify the sound of one instrument, such as a violin.

It involves the ability to know which note being played on a flute is higher. Which sound is louder? Which sound was made by a

bird and which was made by a person whistling? Was the sound made by a jet plane or the wind? How are all of these sounds alike? How are they different? Again, the idea is to develop a mental set for listening to sounds in terms of their similarities and differences.

Once children have developed both the willingness and the skill to identify sounds, they can become more aware of the world around them. They may listen to directions more carefully. They also learn to identify the sound of words.

- "Ball" sounds like "tall" except for the first sound in each word.

- "Ball" sounds like "bell" except for the middle sound in each word.

- "Bell" sounds like "belt" except for the last sound in each word.

Later, when children see letters and hear sounds in reading, the skills learned in sciencing begin to benefit them. They have actually learned phonics skills. Children learn to recognize sounds. They know that sounds, just like objects, have similarities and differences.

Developing physical skills. Physical skills are as basic to reading as are mental skills. Children's eyes must focus properly. They must learn to move their eyes from left to right. Coordination is needed to hold a book, or to turn the page. Children must be able to concentrate on the pictures and the letters. They must be able to find the clues that help them identify letters and words.

All of these are physical skills. They involve small and large muscle coordination and the ability to move one's eyes properly. These skills can be learned by children in sciencing activities. They sort, arrange, and study. They move small objects from one place to another, and combine things. Children learn to concentrate and to search for answers. In this process, they develop important physical skills that help them become better readers later in school.

Developing concepts and vocabulary. Reading is a skill. It helps people learn about things they cannot experience directly. Children should not just be taught to read words. Children should go to school to learn to read for information and pleasure. Reading is not the end product. The information and pleasure is the desired result.

Thus, if reading is to have meaning for a child, the child must see the purpose of that reading. Reading helps a child learn more about concepts (mental pictures). Concepts develop through experience. As a child's experiences become greater, the number of concepts which the child possesses are expanded. The greater the number of concepts children possess the greater are the interests of those children.

In other words, children develop concepts through direct experience. They add meaning to those concepts through reading. When children read with a purpose they usually work harder and learn more.

Children have many experiences in sciencing which lead them to develop new concepts and new interests. Later, when books are available, these children will be able to use these early experiences. Reading will help them answer questions or explain problems that are a part of their experience.

Sciencing also helps a child develop a bigger and better vocabulary. New words are often needed to describe or explain new experiences. The new words can be learned from adults or other children. Sometimes new words are created by children.

In general, when children learn a word they want to remember, they try to use it every chance they get. One might hear four-year-olds talk about rectangles and triangles. If they have a reason they will learn the meanings and use many new words. The key is that they need to have a reason. Experiences gained in sciencing can serve as that reason.

Sciencing can help in meeting the needs of individual children. Anyone who works with children learns that no two are exactly alike.

Parents learn that each of their children is an individual. Each child has likes and dislikes. Each has special skills.

Teachers also learn to recognize that each child is an individual. In a classroom, however, children bring great differences in past experience to each situation. Some come from homes where parents are strict; others come from lenient homes. Some have had great amounts of love; others, no love at all. Some have never been out of the neighborhood in which they were born; others have traveled widely. Some were read to from early infancy and have many books in their homes; others never saw a book. Some have many toys of their own; others, few. Some must compete with ten brothers and sisters; others have none. The point is that different children have had different past experiences and have different present needs. No one approach to learning, no one type of class experience, no one group of learnings can meet the needs of all the children in a class. A teacher must be prepared to meet the varied needs of children with a variety of class experiences.

Sciencing may be the way in which the needs of some individuals are met. Sciencing cannot meet all of their needs, or appeal to every child. However, many children do enjoy sciencing because of the discovery emphasis and the availability of materials. Sciencing is unlike anything else in the school program. The approach used and the ideas stressed may be missing from many school programs. With sciencing, children are given a chance to learn what they like, in a way they like.

In some cases, children develop new skills and interests when exposed to sciencing. They may not have been allowed the freedom to explore in their home. Sciencing gives children an opportunity to manipulate materials and to learn by discovery. It can help uncover the special needs and reveal the special skills of these children.

Some children have never worked alone. They may have been dominated by an older brother or overly concerned parent. The chance to work alone in sciencing may be their first chance to express themselves or discover a special skill. Thus, by appealing to children's interests, encouraging new interests, and providing for variety in a school program, sciencing helps in meeting some of the needs of individuals.

Sciencing contributes to skill development. There are two kinds of skills that are influenced by sciencing. One type involves the skill of investigating — how to go about finding answers to problems. The other type involves skills of manipulation — developing coordination and small muscle skills.

Investigating skills are those described in earlier units as process skills. They are the skills that help one process information. They include observing, classifying, and others. A child who can apply these skills to solve problems has learned something valuable. A person who can make careful and accurate observations can use those skills throughout life. These skills are learned in sciencing but are not used in sciencing alone. They can be used every day in many ways. They can show a person that problems can be solved, often by more than just one method. In addition, skill in using the processes can help one understand that some problems have more than just one right answer.

Motor skills, like process skills, can be learned in sciencing. However, they, too, can be used in many other facets of one's life. Skills of hand-eye coordination can be applied in reading, writing, and sports activities. Small muscle skills also have very wide application. It is important to note that these skills develop as one participates in the sciencing activities. Parents and teachers provide the chance for a child to take part in sciencing. As the child takes part, the skills develop.

Sciencing helps children develop healthy positive feelings about themselves. What can discourage a child more than to consider himself a failure at everything? There are children who are convinced that they will fail at all school activities. They expect to fail and therefore they do fail. There are other children who feel very confident about themselves. They are sure that they can do well at anything they try. They expect to succeed and they usually do succeed.

The difference between the "cannot do" and the "can do" children is their past experience. Those children who have met with past success usually develop a good feeling about themselves. They are not afraid of temporary failure. They attack problems with vigor and think of them as fun challenges.

Those who have met with past failure often think of themselves as poor performers. They think, "What's the use of trying? I'll just fail again." They are afraid of new problems. They try to avoid situations in which they might meet with additional failure.

Sciencing is designed for both kinds of children. There is a variety of activities for those who like to take on and solve problems. For those who are fearful about getting wrong answers many activities are designed to have several correct solutions. These activities are

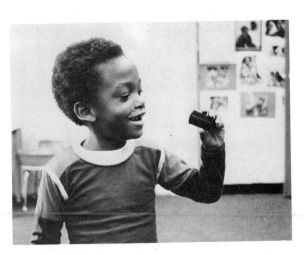

said to be open-ended (no one correct answer; but many proper answers). In addition, many activities are designed so that children set their own goals. They decide what to do, how to do it, and what results they will accept. In a case such as this, a child is likely to succeed.

Children tend to get immediate feedback from sciencing activities. That is, they know right away if their solution works or does not work. They can then share their successes with people who are important to them. It may be that they want a teacher to know how well they have done. Perhaps it is another child or a parent whom they want to inform. They are able to get the recognition they want.

Sciencing tends to seem like a game to children. They don't think of it as working or even as learning. For many children, it is not a serious problem if they make an error in a game. It is a problem if they thought they were showing their "stupidity" in some schoolwork. Thus, children overlook some of their errors in sciencing and continue "playing the game." Eventually, they succeed. They also finally discover that sciencing is, in fact, a learning activity, and they have succeeded in a learning activity.

Children develop an understanding of the world around them in sciencing. What happens to snow when it is heated? What happens to gelatin when it has been brought to a boil and then placed in a very cool place? How does the world look when one looks at it through green cellophane? What happens to a banana when it is allowed to sit in a covered dish on a table for three weeks?

Children can learn answers to these and many more questions about the world in sciencing. They can study the properties of objects and learn to identify solids, liquids, and gases. They can observe objects as these objects change from one form to another or one shape to another.

In addition, children can learn that much of the natural world can be studied and understood by them. Through their own investigations they can find out about nature. They can also begin to understand that many natural things that take place in the world have causes. Children can observe how cause A brings about result B. They can also discover that cause A always brings about result B if all other conditions remain the same.

Some basic needs of children can be satisfied in sciencing. Three- to five-year-olds are

usually curious. Yet, in school, quiet, obedient children are the ones who tend to be rewarded. Excitable, inquisitive ones are punished. Sciencing is designed to recognize and reward children who express their natural curiosity. Children are expected to ask questions. They are expected to investigate and search out answers. Curiosity is encouraged in sciencing. Many children also need to work with other children. They want the chance to exhibit their skills to others. They need recognition both from other children and from adults. Sciencing provides children with an opportunity to work alone and to work with others. In this way a variety of social needs can be satisfied.

Play activities are a basic part of most children's needs. They like to play and they need to express themselves through play. Sciencing activities are very similar to many types of play activities. Children think they are playing — while, in fact, they are learning important skills and concepts.

BENEFITS FOR THE TEACHER

Children benefit from sciencing, but teachers also benefit in a number of ways.

Sciencing helps teachers recognize children's skills. As suggested in an earlier unit, some bright children may go unrecognized by teachers because of the focus on a child's verbal ability. A child who speaks well or reads well is easily recognized by most adults. However, teachers should also realize that some children are good thinkers even if they are not good speakers. How does a teacher discover skillful, nonverbal children? The sciencing activities described in this text provide a teacher with this chance. Children can show discovery skills without having to talk about it. A child can wire an electric circuit without speaking a word.

Teachers who are able to recognize nonverbal children can receive many benefits.

A teacher feels successful when children come into class willingly. The teacher who has helped children recognize that they are skilled has helped them grow. The good feelings children have about themselves can be the direct result of a teacher's efforts. Helping children succeed by helping them recognize their skills can thus become a great reward for teachers. In this way, sciencing can help teachers carry out their job more effectively.

Sciencing helps teachers provide a variety of activities for children. Children, today, are exposed to some highly exciting educational television programs. They watch shows in which numerals leap across the screen. Words and letters appear in an explosion of sounds and sights and then disappear. There are humorous characters and creative sets to attract and hold the children's interests. Something unique is needed if schools are to compete with the mass media for children's attentions. The key seems to be that children do not get actively involved in watching television. They are passive observers. Teachers can therefore benefit if they develop a school program in which children actively participate in learning. One of many activities that lends itself to active participation by children is sciencing. The challenging activities and the direct involvement by the children add variety to the school program.

Sciencing helps teachers develop a rapport with children. Good feelings between a teacher and a child help both in many ways. A teacher who is doing a good job may be a happy, friendly person. The teacher gets to know the children better and is willing to try new teaching approaches.

Children tend to like their teacher if they feel the teacher likes them. Many children learn better in a friendly classroom. But how can warm, friendly relationships be

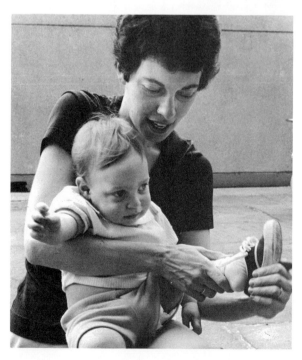

created in a classroom? One way is to produce conditions where teachers and children work together. When they work together they have a chance to communicate in a meaningful way. A more natural relationship can thus grow. When children are involved in sciencing, the teacher can speak with the child. They can talk about the investigation, and discuss the child's feelings. The child and teacher thus develop a rapport.

Another way for a teacher to build better teacher-pupil relations is to help each child succeed in some way in the classroom. The child should know that a job has been done well. Different children do better at different things. Thus, a teacher must provide a variety of activities for children to help each child succeed. Sciencing provides a child with a variety of ways to succeed. It provides the teacher with a variety of ways to help the child succeed. It also helps both teacher and child to recognize this success.

BENEFITS FOR THE SCHOOL

In planning and carrying out sciencing activities teachers can help improve the school program and the school image in a number of ways.

Sciencing can help make schoolwork more interesting. Schools must be designed so that children feel that learning is fun. However, children do not have to be entertained. They do not have to have fun at all times. They should realize that learning and fun can go together.

Sciencing can help schools meet some of the basic needs of children. Because children are so curious, ways must be found to reward curiosity. School activities should be planned which allow children to express their curiosity. Children have a need to feel secure. They must feel accepted in school. Thus, school programs must be created to meet the needs of the children. They should be designed to help children express their natural skills. The programs should also help children extend their skills and learn new ones. They cannot be too hard or too easy for children. The program should help children develop the ability to use discovery methods to make discoveries.

Sciencing is designed to do these things. Before an activity is created, these questions should be asked:

- Does it meet the needs of the children?

- Will it be fun for them?

- Will they be able to do the work asked of them?

- Will they learn something of value?

Sciencing can help a school program become more exciting. It can help the school better meet the needs of children. Children learn valuable knowledge. In all of these ways sciencing benefits the school program and the children.

SUMMARY

Sciencing provides benefits for the child, the teacher, and the school. Children benefit in that (1) sciencing activities provide help in building reading readiness skills; (2) needs of individuals can be better met; (3) special skills can be developed in sciencing; (4) a good feeling about one's self can develop as a result of sciencing experiences; (5) knowledge is acquired; and (6) basic emotional needs can be met.

Teachers benefit because (1) they get more experience in recognizing the skills of each child in their group; (2) they can have more variety in their school program; and (3) they may be able to establish a better rapport with children.

School programs improve because (1) schools can become more interesting places where children enjoy learning and (2) some of the basic needs of children can be better met through sciencing.

SUGGESTED ACTIVITIES

- Prepare a one page essay explaining what sciencing is.

- Tell how children, teachers, and the school program are likely to benefit from sciencing.

REVIEW

A. True or False

If the statement is true, mark T in the blank. If the statement is false, mark F in the blank, and correct the statement.

_____ 1. Sciencing can help a child develop auditory discrimination skills.

_____ 2. Visual discrimination has to do with the sense of touch.

_____ 3. Educators must keep children from developing mental sets.

_____ 4. A child with many well developed sciencing concepts is likely to have an advantage when learning to read.

_____ 5. The needs of individual children are not a concern in sciencing.

_____ 6. Sciencing helps children develop a number of useful skills.

_____ 7. Open-ended sciencing activities always have one specific right answer.

_____ 8. Children must be motivated to study the world around them because they do not become interested in these things by themselves.

_____ 9. Children should not be allowed to mix schoolwork and play.

_____10. Cooperation among children should be encouraged in sciencing.

B. Choose the correct word to complete each statement.

1. It is sad that some people consider learning to be _____ (dull/exciting).   They should be encouraged to think that learning is _____ (fun/difficult).

2. Teachers must find ways to _____ (punish/reward) children for their curiosity.

3. School programs must be designed to help children express their _____ (anger/skills).

4. Sciencing should help children add to their _____ (storehouse of knowledge/fear of the unknown).

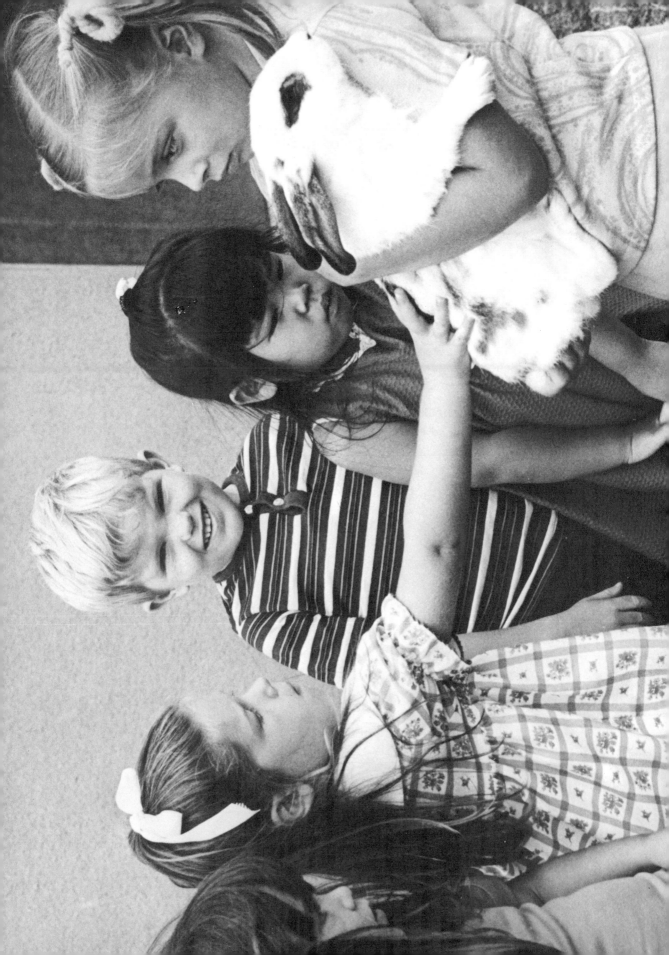

Section II Sciencing Activities

introduction to activities

In Section 1 it was explained that sciencing is made up of three types of activities. The activities are designed to achieve different goals. The reason for having three types of activities is based on the characteristics and needs of the children. Since no two children are exactly alike, a program for three- to five-year-olds should recognize that different children need different activities. Variety in a program for children makes that program more meaningful for children.

Activities to Meet Children's Needs

Sciencing is designed to provide children with a variety of activities that are presented in a variety of ways. For children who need a little more encouragement and direction there is the type of activity called formal sciencing. This is a teacher-directed approach in which children learn by doing. The teachers prepare materials and help children get started. Children do the work.

For children who are self-starters and very interested in investigating scientific ideas there is a type of activity called informal sciencing. In this type of activity children select materials that have been placed in small containers (such as shoe boxes) and try to see what they can discover.

Sometimes something very exciting happens to a young child. The child may want to talk about it or know more about it. If this event is related to science, the activity that follows is called incidental sciencing. Children may see a rainbow and want to know more about rainbows. If frightened by a tornado or rainstorm, children want to know more about these things. These incidents are not planned but are important to children. A good teacher takes advantage of such opportunities and uses them to create an incidental sciencing experience.

Formal Sciencing — Review

This type of sciencing is designed to help children learn skills and then to apply those skills as they learn knowledge. The skills are called *inquiry process skills*. They help children learn how to investigate in a more thorough and accurate way.

These inquiry process skills are:

- Observing: learning to use all of the senses.
- Classifying: learning to sort objects on the basis of some observable properties.
- Communicating: learning to exchange information clearly and accurately.

Basic Skill Development (Inquiry Process Skills)	Basic Knowledge (Science-related information)
Children learn how to <u>observe</u>. Children learn how to <u>communicate</u> accurately about observations they have made. Children learn how to <u>classify</u> objects that they have observed. Children learn how to <u>quantify</u> objects or sets of objects that they have observed and classified.	Properties of objects can be observed and described. Objects can be compared on the basis of similarities and differences. Properties of solids, liquids, and gases can be observed, described, and compared. Objects go through changes in form and shape which can be observed, described, and compared.

Fig. A-1 Order for presentation of activities.

- Quantifying: learning to compare objects on the basis of amount or size; to use numbers and numerals; and to arrange objects in an order.

After children have had some experience with each of these skills, they are ready to apply the skills. The skills are used to help children learn useful knowledge. The information to be learned includes the principles that:

- Objects have properties that can be observed and described.

- Objects can be compared on the basis of their similarities and differences.

- Solids, liquids, and gases have properties that can be observed and compared.

- Objects go through changes in form and shape which can be observed.

There is a logical order in which the skills are developed and then applied to the body of information. Figure A-1 shows the order in which activities can be presented.

Formal Sciencing Activities

The following activities are presented as examples of the kinds of formal sciencing lessons children can experience. The plans are provided as suggestions of what can be done with children.

Each lesson begins with a brief statement about the lesson. This is followed by one or more behavioral objectives. (These objectives are only suggested learning outcomes. Children should not be forced to learn, but rather encouraged to investigate.) The materials needed and the amounts are indicated. A procedure is given and each lesson concludes with comments. These comments are suggestions based on the results of field testing of the activities.

All activities were tested with three-, four-, and five-year-old children. It was found that some activities seemed to be more appropriate for one age level than another. Figures A-2 and A-3, pages 85 and 86, list all of the activities by category and appropriate age level.

Type of Activity	Suggested Age Groups		
	3 yr. olds	4 yr. olds	5 yr. olds
A. Observing			
1. Color clues	X	X	X
2. Matching colors	X	X	X
3. Mixing and matching colors	X	X	X
4. Color changes	X	X	X
5. The effect of white	X	X	X
6. Melting		X	X
7. Identifying a substance by its odor	X	X	X
8. A touching experience	X	X	X
9. Select-a-shape	X	X	X
10. How wet is wet?		X	X
11. Matching sounds	X	X	X
12. Swish, rattle, clunk		X	X
13. Picture clues			X
14. Only the shadow knows			X
15. Using all of the senses (Part I)	X	X	X
16. Using all of the senses (Part II)	X	X	X
B. Classifying			
1. Who's got the button?		X	X
2. A leaf scavenger hunt		X	X
3. Getting the feel of things		X	X
4. Sorting in the mystery box		X	X
5. Shape up bingo			X
C. Quantifying			
1. Numerals and numbers			X
2. Cardinals and ordinals			X
3. Sets and numbers			X
4. Which has more?			X
5. Arranging objects in order			X
D. Communicating			
1. The property game			X
2. The "blind" teacher			X
3. Things we can hear but cannot see			X
4. Name the speaker			X
5. I can't hear you!			X

Fig. A-2 Process activities

Type of Activity	Suggested Age Groups		
	3 yr. olds	4 yr. olds	5 yr. olds
A. Describing properties			
1. Comparisons	X	X	X
2. More comparisons	X	X	X
3. Sorting by properties	X	X	X
4. Counting sets of objects		X	X
5. Describing this and that		X	X
B. Properties of solids, liquids, and gases			
1. A look at some solids		X	X
2. Mix 'n match		X	X
3. Fizz-bang!		X	X
4. The candy maker	X	X	X
5. Shells and more shells	X	X	X
6. The shape of things		X	X
7. Telling about air	X	X	X
8. Disappearing liquids	X	X	X
9. It shivers and quivers		X	X
10. Mystery boxes			X
C. Similarities and differences			
1. A pirate treasure hunt		X	X
2. Which are alike?		X	X
3. Who made that sound?			X
D. Combining, rearranging, and disassociating objects			
1. Pancakes perfect			X
2. Food for thought	X	X	X
3. Play with clay		X	X
4. Mixing and unmixing			X

Fig. A-3 Content activities

OBSERVING 1: COLOR CLUES

This activity is designed to help children observe and recognize colors and match objects on the basis of color similarity.

Objectives

At the end of this activity children should be able to

- Sort a variety of materials according to color.
- Identify the color of an object as red, green, blue, yellow, orange, purple, brown, or black.

Materials

Each child receives

- A small bag of materials colored—red, green, yellow, blue, orange, purple, brown, and black. These may be pieces of material, yarn, paint chips, construction paper, buttons, or a combination of these things.
- A tray

Procedure

1. Distribute a tray and a bag of materials to each child.
2. Let the children investigate the contents of the bag. Suggest that the objects in the bag are alike in some way.
3. Accept all of the responses. When a color is mentioned, hold up several objects of that color and ask the children to find something in their set of materials that is also that color.
4. Proceed through the other colors in the same way. Then ask the children if they can group all of the things that are of the same color in their set.
5. As a follow-up, have a color object hunt. Designate color tables by placing a paper of the given color on that table. Children can choose the color they wish to work with. Many objects of that color should be distributed around the room. Have children search for objects of the given color and place them on the correct table.

Comments

Observe the children as they sort materials. Reinforce color names whenever possible. Crayons are useful for identification of colors.

OBSERVING 2: MATCHING COLORS

Children match colors from memory and play a game of color dominoes in this activity.

Objectives

At the end of this activity children should be able to

- Identify a series of colors from memory.
- Match colors when shown a similar color and name the colors involved.

Materials

Each child receives

- A set of 10 paint chip cards.
- A master set of cards.
- A set of color dominoes.

Procedure

For matching card game:

1. Distribute a set of cards to each child. Place a master set of cards on a table where the children can see it.
2. Select a child to act as caller. The caller selects one card from the master set and states the name of the color to the group. The other children must find a card of that color in their pack of cards.
3. When a child can match the master card with one in his pack, the card is returned to the pack.
4. Continue playing until all of the master cards have been distributed. The child with the most master cards can select cards and direct the activity the next time it is carried out.

For domino game:

1. Distribute color domino pieces to the children. Play in a group around a table.
2. In order for a child to place a domino on the table, the colors must match and the child must be able to name the color. The first child to get all dominoes on the table is the winner.

Comments

Color paint chips are available at most paint suppliers. Dominoes can be homemade using tagboard or other stiff material.

OBSERVING 3: MIXING AND MATCHING COLORS

In this activity children observe primary colors and various shades of these colors.

Objectives

At the end of this activity children should be able to

- Identify shades of the primary colors.
- Match different intensities of the same color.

Materials

Each child receives

- A piece of cardboard on which have been mounted strips of paint chips, for example: basic blue and a row of shades of blue, or basic red and shades of red.

- An assortment of chips which have been cut from paint chip cards so that each chip can be handled individually. Each chip matches one of the colors included in the mounted color strips. Place the strips in a grab bag.

Procedure

1. Each child receives one color strip and a set of six individual paint chips drawn from a grab bag. Children should first match individual chips to those on their strips.
2. They may then return individual chips to the grab bag and select a new chip for each one returned.
3. The goal is to try to match the entire strip with individual paint chips.
4. Another activity involves naming the basic color when a shade of that color is observed.

Comments

Paint chips can also be used for an art or design activity. Encourage children to identify the basic color related to each chip and to name the colors. Do not stress the names of the color variations, but some children might be interested in names such as lime, peach, hazel, or shocking pink.

OBSERVING 4: COLOR CHANGES

Children usually like mixing paints and food coloring to make new colors. This activity provides them with the opportunity to combine a variety of colors in order to see all the various shades and new colors they can obtain.

Objectives

At the end of this activity children should be able to

- Combine red, blue, and yellow colors in various ways to make green, orange, and purple.

- Name the colors red, blue, yellow, green, orange, and purple.

Materials

Each child receives

- Eight small pill bottles half filled with water.

- Red, blue, and yellow tempera paint or food coloring.

- Three eye droppers and eight stirrers.

- Waxed paper or newspaper.

Procedure

1. Distribute pill bottles, stirrers, colors, and eye droppers. Make sure paper is spread on tables or on the floor.

2. Let children examine the materials and investigate what happens when colors are mixed.

3. After an initial period ask the children to see how many different colors they can make from red, blue, and yellow.

4. Work with individual children. Ask them to name the colors that result from the mixing.

5. A demonstration using large gallon jars in which colors are mixed might follow children's investigations. Again, naming all colors is good learning reinforcement for the children.

Comments

Children can paint using the temperas. This may be a very messy lesson. Have sponges and buckets of water handy.

OBSERVING 5: THE EFFECT OF WHITE

This activity is designed to extend children's observational skills by encouraging them to make finer discriminations of various similar colors.

Objectives

At the end of this activity children should be able to

- Mix various amounts of white paint to colors, and observe the change in the colors.
- Show how a color can be made lighter by adding white paint to it.

Materials

Each child receives

- A tablespoon.
- Paintbrush and newsprint.
- A small dish or cup of white tempera paint.
- A dish of paint — one color selected from the following: red, green, yellow, orange, blue, purple, brown, and black.
- A styrofoam egg carton (for mixing paints).

Procedure

1. Distribute materials and suggest that all materials be used.
2. As children mix their colors, discuss the terms light and dark with children but do not dwell on the terms. Children may want to make a painting using the various shades of their color.
3. For a follow-up activity, the children could make a group mural with each child adding something to the painting. After the children add their colors, they can tell each other about the colors — one is dark red or light red or pink, and how they made the color they decided to use.

Comments

Listen to children's comments to see if they realize that adding white lightens the shade of the basic color.

OBSERVING 6: MELTING

In this activity children in small groups observe changes in the shape, size, and color of a variety of common substances.

Objectives

At the end of this activity children should be able to

- Identify changes in color, shape, and size of substances used.
- Recognize that some substances change greatly when heated, while others change very little.

Materials

Each group receives

- A hot plate, hot pads, and trivet.
- Five aluminum trays from TV dinners.
- Approximately equal-size cubes of bread, margarine, beeswax, chocolate, and ice.

Procedure

NOTE: When the hot plate is being used, be sure the children do not burn themselves.

1. Allow the children to examine and identify the substances being used.
2. Then place each of the five materials in a compartment of the aluminum tray and place on a hot plate that has been preheated.
3. Ask the children to observe and describe what is happening. If no one describes color, shape, or size changes, ask the group about these things.
4. Next, melt two equal-size cubes of margarine, one which is very cold (frozen, if possible) and the other which has been allowed to warm at room temperature for a period of time.
5. Place a large and a small cube of ice in a TV tray and heat them. What happens?
6. Finally, heat one tray on the hot plate and chill a second tray in a refrigerator or on a window sill (if it is cold outside).
7. Place both trays on a table near the children. (Be sure they do not touch the trays). Put equal-size cubes of chocolate, ice, and margarine in each.
8. Have the children observe what happens.

Comments

Children may try to explain differences in melting rates and changes in color or shape. Accept their explanations but encourage them to think of other explanations of the observations they made. This is a demonstration activity. In order to hold children's attentions, the materials must be prepared in advance. Things should move quickly so that children do not become bored.

OBSERVING 7: IDENTIFYING A SUBSTANCE BY ITS ODOR

This activity is built around the sense of smell. Children first try to match odors directly, and then indirectly in a more challenging way.

Objectives

At the end of this activity children should be able to

- Match three substances with distinctive odors.
- Match one unknown substance to one of three known substances using only the sense of smell.

Materials

Each child receives

- Six opaque cups (covered on all sides with aluminum foil): two containing lemon juice, two almond extract, and two very diluted onion juice. Each cup can be identified with a numeral, a letter, or a color.

Each group of six children receives

- Three "known" liquids in a cup: vanilla, pineapple juice, and peppermint extract.
- An "unknown" in a covered cup (one for each child: the unknown should, of course, be one of the three known substances).

Procedure

1. Distribute the set of six covered cups to each child and ask the children to use their sense of smell to find out all they can about what is in the cups.
2. After the children have had some time to explore, ask them to match cups that seem to smell alike.
3. Observe the children's behavior and discuss the results with individuals.
4. As a follow-up activity, let the children spend about five minutes smelling the three known liquids. Then give each child an unknown set. The child must identify which known liquid it smells like, without smelling the knowns again.
5. Encourage the children to share problems encountered in this activity.

Comments

This may be a difficult activity for some children. Do not spend too much time discussing this activity. Sciencing should be child-centered, not teacher-centered.

OBSERVING 8: A TOUCHING EXPERIENCE

In this activity children use a touch box to try to observe and match materials using only the sense of touch.

Objectives

At the end of this activity children should be able to

• Match objects on the basis of texture.

Materials

• One or more touch boxes for the class.

• Pairs of three-inch squares of fabric: 2 pairs each of burlap, wool, cotton, acetate, satin, corduroy, netting, velveteen, felt, fur (not all of these may be available; other materials can be substituted).

Procedure

1. Scramble the various fabric squares inside the touch box.
2. Ask children to reach into the box with both hands and without looking, bring out two squares of fabric that feel the same.
3. Continue this until the box is empty.

Comments

Most fabric stores sell remnants. Many sell fabrics in quantities of 1/8 yard.

To make a touch box: Close the top of a cardboard box, wrap the entire box in wrapping paper. Cut two three-inch holes in one side of the box. Attach about an eight-inch length of shirt sleeve to the side of the box at each hole with masking tape. Project each sleeve inside-out in the box. Insert a six inch piece of plastic at the end of each sleeve to make the sleeve adjustable.

This activity is best carried out with a very small group of children — not more than three or four.

OBSERVING 9: SELECT-A-SHAPE

In this activity children further develop their observational skills by coordinating their sense of touch with their ability to perceive shape.

Objectives

At the end of this activity children should be able to

- Select an object from several objects based on shape. The child cannot see the objects but can touch them.
- Name at least two shapes.

Materials

Each group of children receives

- Wooden or cardboard box like that used in Observing 8. Six different shapes made out of wood (or cardboard) are glued to the top in a circular pattern. Shapes used for this box are a rectangle, a star, a triangle, a diamond, a square, and a circle.
- A spinner for the box top, made and attached so that it spins freely.
- Two sets each of the six shapes (identical to those on the top of the box), placed inside the box.

Procedure

1. Place the spin-a-shape box in the middle of the room. Some children will be drawn to the box and will try to discover its purpose.
2. Do not answer questions right away, but encourage the children to use the box in whatever way they choose. If desired, explain the procedure to a small group.
3. The box should be left in the room so that all children may work with it individually for as long as they wish.
4. After a period of time, ask if some children would like to play a game called spin-a-shape. About four children can play the game at one time.
5. After spinning the shape, a child must reach into the box and find the shape before the teacher counts to five. If the shape is found, the child can keep it until the game is over.
6. After the game has ended, see which child has the most shapes.
7. Encourage children to name the shapes on the box. It may be necessary to tell them such names as rectangle, triangle, and square.

Comments

The construction of the spin-a-shape box is similar to the touch box except a spinner is placed on top. The same box can be used if a removable-shape spinner is used. A piece of aluminum or a wooden dowel can be used for the spinner. Remember, the spinner must spin quite freely.

Make the box colorful. The attractiveness of the box and its shapes on top can serve to encourage children to try the spin-a-shape.

OBSERVING 10: HOW WET IS WET?

This activity is based on the sense of touch, but differs from the preceding activities in that the child is asked to touch liquids to see which are alike and which are different.

Objectives

At the end of this activity children should be able to

- Identify several liquids using the sense of touch.
- Describe how liquids feel alike and how they feel different.

Materials

Each child receives

- A small cup of each of the following: cooking oil, water, and a solution of water and detergent.
- Paper towels.

Each group of four children receives

- Plastic containers half filled with the same liquids used above (freezer containers work well).
- A curtain and apparatus designed to conceal the containers of liquid from the child's sight.
- Paper towels and a basin of water for cleaning up.

Procedure

1. Let each child investigate one set of liquids. Tell the children that they will be asked to work with the liquids in a short while without being able to see them.
2. Then work in small groups. Place six plastic containers behind a curtained apparatus. Each container should be half filled with one of the three liquids in the following way: 3 containers of soapy water, 2 containers of cooking oil, and 1 container of water.
3. The children in each group may touch the liquids as much as they want. The group should try to decide how many containers of what liquid were behind the curtain.
4. Encourage the children to describe how the liquids feel different. Also ask them to consider how they know which liquid is which.

Comments

The curtained apparatus may be any of the following: a small puppet stage, a cardboard box with one side missing, a small table with curtains all around.

Be prepared for a mess. Liquids spill very easily.

OBSERVING 11: MATCHING SOUNDS

In this activity children are given the opportunity to match sounds heard on a tape recorder with instruments in the classroom.

Objectives

At the end of this activity children should be able to

- Point to the instrument whose sound is being heard on a tape recording.
- Identify two instruments when they are heard together on a tape recording.

Materials

The materials to be used are

- One tape recorder and tape.
- Common instruments such as a tambourine, triangle, cymbals, recorder, Autoharp.®

Procedure

1. Prerecord the sounds of various instruments individually.
2. Then record the sounds in pairs.
3. Work in small groups so that each child can hold one of the instruments heard on the recording as the children hear the taped sound. If they think they are holding the same instrument as on the recording they must try to duplicate the sound. Let children help one another.
4. Repeat the activity letting the children hear pairs of instruments. They are again to reproduce the sounds they hear. Encourage children to discuss what they heard and whether the sounds they played were like the recorded sounds.
5. Let the children organize a band if they wish. Instruments can be supplemented by rubber band twanging, hand clapping, or blowing over the tops of bottles.

Comments

This activity can succeed only if the instruments used in the recording are available in the class.

OBSERVING 12: SWISH, RATTLE, CLUNK

This is an activity designed to make children aware of the sense of sound as an observational skill.

Objectives

At the end of this activity children should be able to

- Use the sense of sound to match various sounds that are similar.

Materials

Each pair of children receives

- Two plastic bottles or baby food jars made opaque by covering them with contact paper or by painting them. Each bottle should contain one large bolt.
- Two containers filled with the same amount of sugar.
- Two containers filled with the same amount of split peas.

All bottles must be covered in some way. Curious children can then peak at the contents after they have matched the similar sounds.

Procedure

1. Distribute the materials. Encourage the children to investigate their sets of materials to find out what they can about the materials — particularly about the contents of the bottles.

2. They may not open the bottles or look inside. Ask them which bottles contain the same objects or materials. See if they can give reasons for their answers.

Comments

These materials can be used to introduce the idea of loud and soft sounds. Make sure that the bottles are opaque.

OBSERVING 13: PICTURE CLUES

In this activity children try to identify an object after seeing part of that object.

Objectives

At the end of this activity children should be able to

- Name observable clues that helped them identify an object.
- Recognize differences between observations and guesses.

Materials

The materials to be used are

- A magazine or other pictures of common objects.
- An overlay setup (described under procedure).

Procedure

1. Prepare the picture overlays in the following manner: Paste one picture on a piece of tagboard or other firm backing material. Place over the picture a series of masks (cutouts that reveal more and more of the picture as each is removed) that are attached to the hard backing in such a way that they can be flipped over or removed.

2. The mask closest to the picture should reveal about half of the object. The next mask should reveal slightly less than half and so on. The top mask should reveal only a small section of the object.

3. As children try to name the object in the picture, work with them on the concept of guessing versus observation. For instance, ask them whether they can observe a cow on the picture or if they think that it is a cow because of some physical characteristics.

4. When children think they know what the object is, let them state their observations. Ask them to tell why they think the object is what they have named.

5. Remove any remaining masks and ask the rest of the children who are participating if they agree with the statements and why.

6. Have a number of pictures ready for any one session.

Comments

A sequence of pictures showing a continuous action can be used. Some pictures can be covered. Children should observe what the covered pictures show. This activity is best carried out in very small groups — two or three children and one adult or by individual children working with one adult.

OBSERVING 14: ONLY THE SHADOW KNOWS

In this activity children try to identify an object by observing its shadow made on a screen.

Objectives

At the end of this activity children should be able to

- Identify a common object by observing its shadow.
- Compare a shadow to the actual object.

Materials

Each group of children should have

- One shadow box or screen.
- A number of objects with distinct and recognizable shapes, for example: star, fork, spoon, or telephone. Objects can be real or artificial.
- Pictures or sketches of objects used.

Procedure

1. Bright sunlight or light from an artificial source behind a screen creates a shadow on the screen when an object is placed between the light source and the screen. If a shadow box is used, two light sources are needed.

2. Hold the objects behind the screen at unusual angles or directly upright. Ask the children to name the object, and why they think it is what they have named.

3. Also have the children match pictures of objects with the shadows observed. Children should be informed that they are not observing the object directly. They are seeing a shadow.

4. Ask children to name the senses they use to make their observation.

5. Ask them to find a way to use more than one sense in this investigation.

Comments

Let the children play with the shadow box or screen. Each child can become involved in leading this activity. Use a wide variety of common objects.

This activity should be quite brief when carried out with a group. However, when only two or three children are involved the activity can continue for a longer period.

OBSERVING 15: USING ALL OF THE SENSES (PART I)

In this activity children try to use all five senses to make observations.

Objectives

At the end of this activity children should be able to

- Make ten observations about the object they are studying.
- Name the parts of the body used to make observations such as eyes, nose, ears, hands, and tongue.

Materials

Each child receives

- One hard candy wrapped in cellophane.
- A piece of sandpaper.
- A cup of water.
- A magnifying glass.
- A piece of paper toweling.
- A small plastic or cardboard tray.

The entire group receives

- A cassette tape recorder and blank tape.
- Pictures of a nose, eyes, tongue, ear, and hand.

Procedure

1. Place all of the materials for each child on a tray.
2. Distribute the trays and ask the children to study the objects on the tray. They can do anything they want to the objects. Do not stress the idea of using all of the senses. Merely ask the children to make as many observations as they can.
3. Have the tape recorder placed in a corner of the room. A helper can assist in operating the tape recorder, if necessary.
4. Tape record some of the children's observations.
5. Play taped observations for the group. For each observation record the sense (or the part of the body) used.
6. Let children add observations that were not recorded. Ask children for evidence to back up their observations.
7. If time permits, repeat the investigation using a slice of carrot, celery, or potato.
8. Now discuss the use of all five senses in making observations.

Comments

Some orderly way of allowing children to tape should be worked out in advance. Children should be cautioned not to shout into the recorder.

OBSERVING 16: USING ALL OF THE SENSES (PART II)

This activity is an extension or continuation of Observing 15. Again children try to use all five senses in making observations.

Objectives

At the end of this activity children should be able to

- Name the five senses.
- Make ten observations about the system they are studying.
- Name the parts of the body used to make observations.

Materials

Each child receives

- A cup of warm water and a cup into which an ice cube has been placed. The ice cube should be made with food-colored water and contain a small cherry or a piece of banana.
- A plastic ruler.
- A plastic spoon.
- A thermometer.
- A magnifying glass.
- Paper towels.
- A piece of string.
- A tape recorder or other means of recording information shared in a discussion.

Procedure

1. Give each child a tray of materials. Ask the children to make as many observations as they can.

2. After about five minutes pair the children into groups of two. Ask the children to share their observations with one another.

3. After another five minutes recombine children into groups of four. Again, ask the children to share observations and to look for new observations.

4. At this point, remind the children about the five senses. After a short time ask those children who are interested to gather around to discuss observations. Let the children do the talking. The discussion can be started by asking for a volunteer to give one or more observations. Have the children add to the list. It may be useful to tape record the discussion or record in some way the children's findings.

Comments

Some children enjoy watching ice melt. Others may become bored after a while. Some children can be allowed to do another activity and return for the discussion period.

During the discussion it is important that teachers give the children a chance to speak out. If the children are slow to contribute, be patient. Once the children start talking, they will all want a chance to participate.

CLASSIFYING 1: WHO'S GOT THE BUTTON?

This is an activity designed to let children sort a set of buttons in at least two different ways.

Objectives

At the end of this activity children should be able to

- Sort a set of buttons according to a single property of their own choosing.
- Sort the same set of buttons in another way.
- Sort a set of buttons according to a predetermined property — for example, color.

Materials

Each child receives

- A set of buttons of various sizes, colors, and shapes.
- A tray.
- A set of 20 buttons: 5 red, 5 blue, 5 green, 5 yellow, and a tray divided into 4 sections. One section contains a red marking, one a blue marking, one a green marking, and one a yellow marking.

Procedure

1. Distribute the sets of buttons and trays. Give no directions at first. Let children play with the buttons.
2. After a while, ask the children to sort the buttons. Walk around the room and discuss with the children how they sorted their buttons.
3. Ask the children to find another way to sort the buttons, but do not tell them what to do or specify a scheme for sorting.
4. Collect the materials.
5. Distribute a second set of buttons consisting of 5 red, 5 blue, 5 green, and 5 yellow buttons. Also distribute a tray divided into four sections. Each section should be marked with one of the four colors of the buttons.
6. Without any explanation, observe what the children do. If some children need assistance, explain that the buttons are to be sorted.

Comments

Closure is not necessary. Observe what the children do with their buttons. Talk with individuals about their sorting procedures. Be careful not to force a classification scheme on a child at the start of this activity. Give the children enough time to proceed on their own.

CLASSIFYING 2: A LEAF SCAVENGER HUNT

In this activity children are given a chance to collect leaves and to classify them in any way they choose.

Objectives

At the end of this activity children should be able to

- Classify leaves according to one self-selected characteristic.
- Arrange leaves according to one teacher-selected property — shape.

Materials

Each child receives

- Ten leaves collected on a nature walk. If possible, the leaves should represent a variety of species.
- A large sheet of construction paper.
- Library paste.
- Paper bag for collecting leaves.

Procedure

NOTE: This activity is best conducted in the autumn when leaves are on the ground. Take the children on a nature walk and ask them to collect a variety of leaves.

1. Have the children arrange their leaves in some order. Several children might like to paste their leaves onto a piece of construction paper after having arranged them in an order.

2. Using duplicate leaves or leaves collected at some other time, ask the children to arrange their leaves according to shape. Let the children decide how they will determine differences in shape. Discuss with individuals what they are doing.

Comments

Encourage children to try as they sort leaves to observe how leaves are shaped. A discussion of the meaning of shape may be necessary.

CLASSIFYING 3: GETTING THE FEEL OF THINGS

Children sort a series of cutout shapes on the basis of shape and texture. They are given a chance to work with a variety of materials that feel very different from one another.

Objectives

At the end of this activity children should be able to

- Sort objects by texture.
- Sort objects by shape.
- Sort objects by a combination of texture and shape.

Materials

Each child receives

- Four triangles (one satin, one cotton, one wool, one burlap).
- Four circles (same four materials as above).
- Four squares (same four materials as above).
- Four irregular shapes (same four materials as above).
- Grab box containing additional pieces of cloth made up of the 4 materials. However, each piece of material is shaped like a rectangle or an oval.

Procedure

1. Distribute the materials.
2. Ask the children to sort their materials.
3. After each child has classified the materials, ask the child to take out eight more pieces of cloth from a grab box. Have the child sort those objects into the groups already created.
4. Have the children sort the materials in as many ways as they can. Encourage individual children to describe their pieces of material. They should also be encouraged to discuss how they sorted the materials.

Comments

This is an easy activity for most of the children. Some need to be encouraged to think of several ways of classifying a set of objects. They tend to think of one property or one idea and do not think about others. Help children see the many possibilities for sorting the objects in different ways.

CLASSIFYING 4: SORTING IN THE MYSTERY BOX

In this activity children classify sixteen objects in a box divided into four sections without being able to see the objects.

Objectives

At the end of this activity children should be able to

- Sort a set of objects by shape.
- Sort a set of objects without being able to directly see those objects.

Materials

Each group of children receives

- A cardboard box closed on all sides. This box should have a hole on each of the 4 sides and a sleeve extending out of each hole. In addition, the inside should be partitioned into quarters.

- A bag containing
  Four circular objects such as ping pong balls, golf balls, or marbles.
  Four flat round objects such as a wooden circle, plastic can cover or lid.
  Four rectangular pieces such as wood or plastic shapes.
  Four cubes such as dice, or wooden cubes.

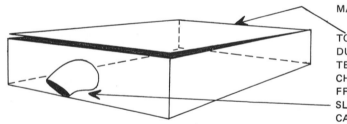

MAKING THE BOX:

TOP OPENS — BUT IS KEPT CLOSED DURING ACTIVITY. PARTITIONS EXTEND 1/2 WAY UP IN THE BOX SO THAT CHILDREN CAN EASILY MOVE OBJECTS FROM ONE SECTION TO ANOTHER. SLEEVE IS PASTED TO BOX SO CHILDREN CAN'T PEEK INTO HOLE.

Procedure

1. The objectives of this activity are best achieved by children working alone. The box should be placed in an area where the work is to be done. The objects should be put into one section of the box.

2. Children sort the objects by placing them into one of the four sections of the box. Ask each child to explain the method used for sorting. Observe the criteria being used by each child for sorting the objects.

Comments

A box such as a beer case is ideal for this activity. The case can be covered with wallpaper, contact paper, or other colorful material. In this way, the box is attractive as well as functional.

CLASSIFYING 5: SHAPE UP BINGO

In this activity, the children sort one set of cards according to shape and another set of cards according to color. They then play bingo with their set of cards using 3x3 bingo cards.

Objectives

At the end of this activity children should be able to

- Sort a set of cards by shape.
- Sort a set of cards by color.
- Combine one color and one shape.

Materials

Each child receives

- A set of 10 cards in four assorted shapes and 6 colors (red, blue, green, orange, yellow, brown).

- A bingo card (3x3 matrix).

1	2	3
4	5	6
7	8	9

- A set of master cards for caller. Each of these cards contains a number, a shape, and a color.

- Packets in which to store sets of cards.
- Markers.

Procedure

1. Distribute a set of shape cards to each child. Let the child sort the cards in any way desired.
2. After a while, ask the children to find a useful way to sort the cards. Explain the rules of bingo and distribute a bingo card to each child.
3. Using the master set of calling cards, call out the number, shape, and color to be covered. If a child has a card containing the shape and color called, the child places a marker on the numeral called.
4. Play until a child has filled a card.

Comments

Make as many sets of cards as needed for a class. They should be made of cardboard and covered with saran wrap. It may be useful to cut out cardboard shapes and paste them on a card. The shapes will then be slightly raised from the card. This helps a child feel as well as see the shapes.

Use a magic marker or other felt tip pen to color the shapes. Children should each receive about ten cards. Because each child's set of cards is made up of a different number of each shape, the children must be alert to the colors and shapes on their set. If the caller calls yellow triangle on square two, it is possible the child may not have a yellow triangle left on the cards.

QUANTIFYING 1: NUMERALS AND NUMBERS

In this activity children will match objects on a one-to-one basis and place the correct number of objects into a small can marked with one numeral.

Objectives

At the end of this activity children should be able to

- Identify the numerals one through ten.
- Name the numerals one through ten.
- Match sets of one to ten objects with the numerals one through ten.

Materials

Each child receives

- Pipe cleaners (in various colors). For example, one red, two blue, three green, four yellow, five white pipe cleaners, etc.
- Ten small cans (with ten colored numerals): can #1 — red numeral, can #2 — blue numeral, can #3 — green numeral, etc.

Procedure

1. Distribute sets of pipe cleaners. Ask children to sort the pipe cleaners by color and to count each subset.
2. Have children match pipe cleaner color and numerical color and place the cleaners in appropriate cans. Work on names of numerals with the children and on the number of pipe cleaners represented by that numeral.
3. When children recognize the numerals 1 to 5, begin work on numerals 6 to 10. Distribute sets of straws (6 red, 7 blue, 8 green, 9 yellow, and 10 white). Have the children place straws in appropriate cans. Count the straws and note numerals.

Comments

Bright colors should be used. Numerals color and pipe cleaner color should be very similar if not identical. Small frozen orange juice cans can be used for this. Be certain to remove any metal fragments or burrs from cans before using them. It may be necessary to work with children one at a time for this activity.

QUANTIFYING 2: CARDINALS AND ORDINALS

This activity is designed to acquaint children with numerals and numerical order.

Objectives

At the end of this activity children should be able to

- Place numeral cards in numerical order.
- Use ordinal words (for example, the words first, second, third) to express order.
- Follow directions involving use of ordinal words.

Materials

The materials to be used are

- Numeral cards 1 through 5.
- Charts of magazine pictures showing order by age, height, and size.
- Animals for flannelboard.
- Flannelboard.
- Five large objects, such as toys which may be found in the classroom.

Procedure

1. Place five chairs in front of the group.
2. Give five children numeral cards and ask them to sit in the chairs in order, first from left to right, then from right to left.
3. Exchange numeral cards and have the children rearrange themselves accordingly.
4. Place five large objects on the floor and have the children place the numeral cards beside the objects in order.
5. Use the flannelboard and pin up animals. Have the children place numeral cards under figures while the teacher introduces ordinal words by saying: "The cow is first, the horse is second, the pig is third," and so on.
6. Give children paper on which five circles have been drawn. Ask the children to color the first one purple, second green, and so on.

Comments

This is a structured teaching lesson. It is useful to work with a few children at one time. If a child becomes frustrated and wants to leave the group, let that child do another activity. Encourage those who already know numerals to help others who do not.

QUANTIFYING 3: SETS AND NUMBERS

This activity is designed to introduce a child to the concept of sets of objects and numbers of a set.

Objectives

At the end of this activity children should be able to

- Identify various sets of objects and speak of them as a set.
- Name the members of a set of objects.

Materials

- Toy dishes and silverware.
- Toy cars and trucks.
- Doll furniture.
- Doll clothes.
- Dominoes and/or checkers.
- Blocks.
- Toy train tracks.
- Crayons, paints, or colored chalk.

Procedure

1. Arrange the various sets of objects so that each set is distinct and clear.
2. Ask children to look at objects and try to find out why certain things are grouped together.
3. Ask children to name the members of the various sets. Point out that sets consist of members — although some sets are empty (have no members).
4. Ask children to find other sets around the classroom, for example, windows, tables, chairs, clothing in coatroom, glasses, dishes, and so on. Encourage the children to name the members of each set.

Comments

This is another highly teacher-directed activity. Some children will not be able to identify sets or name the members of a set. They may need a great deal of practice in these complex concepts before they learn them — although they may understand what is taking place in the activity.

QUANTIFYING 4: WHICH HAS MORE?

This activity is an example of a concept called *conservation of quantity*. Children explore some materials and try to follow simple directions. They change the shapes of some objects but do not increase or decrease the total amount of material they have been given. They are asked to decide whether objects are larger or smaller as a result of the changes they have made. Children who are three, four, and five years old are generally not expected to conserve quantity; that is, most of them will believe that changing an object's shape also changes the amount of material in that object.

Objectives

This activity differs from most of the others included in this group. All that is desired is to show children the relationship between shape and amount. A change in shape does not always indicate a change in amount.

Materials

Each child (or pair of children) receives the following sets of materials. The children should be given one set of materials at a time.

- Set A. Two shoe boxes each containing six wooden blocks.
- Set B. Sixteen plastic (or small metal) dishes; two sheets of paper (dots on paper indicate where dishes should be placed).
- Set C. Two plastic cups and an aluminum pie tin or other low-sided container; water.
- Set D. Two equal-sized pieces of plasticine.
- Set E. A set of twenty-four building blocks (all blocks should be the same size).

Procedure

Children can work alone or in pairs. The entire group can use the same types of materials at the same time, or activities can be individualized.

Children can work alone at their own pace. Children may choose any set of materials as a starting point. They should be encouraged to do all the activities in one set before moving to the next set. In addition, they should be encouraged to try each of the sets. Instructions on how to use sets can be given in each (and possibly all) of the following ways:

- Tell children, one at a time or in small groups, what to do with a set of materials they have chosen.
- Provide a cassette tape and a recorder with directions for using each set of materials.
- Small picture cards on which drawings of what to do can be provided.
- Photographs of children using the materials can be pasted in order into a small booklet.

All children can work with the same types of materials. Each child should have a set of materials. Therefore, large numbers of materials are needed. In addition, teachers must find a way to pass around materials without long delays. Placing sets of materials in color-coded shoe boxes is one way of doing this. Sets of materials can also be placed on cardboard or plastic trays.

Children can work in pairs. Each pair of children should have their own set of materials. Pairs may be allowed to choose the set of materials or may be given a set by the teacher. If pairs choose their sets of materials, teachers should provide instructions for using the sets.

Procedure for Set A

Two identical shoe boxes should be provided. Six blocks are piled in one corner of one of the boxes. In the other box six blocks exactly the same size as those in box one are spread around. Children should be allowed to compare the blocks. They can take blocks out of the boxes. They can build with them, but they must return the blocks to the same positions they found them.

They should decide whether there are more blocks in box one, more in box two, or the same number in each box. Dots or other marks should be placed in box two so children know where to place the blocks when they are finished examining them.

Procedure for Set B

Children are given two sets of identical dishes (unbreakable). There are eight dishes in each set. They are also given two large sheets of paper. The papers have markers that show the children where to place the dishes. Children then compare the dishes on sheet one and sheet two. Are there more dishes in the tall stack on sheet one? Are there more dishes on sheet two? Are there the same number of dishes on each sheet?

 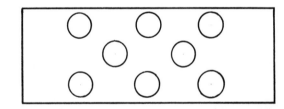

SHEET 1 — 8 DISHES TO BE STACKED IN ONE PLACE.   SHEET 2 — 8 DISHES TO BE SPREAD OUT OVER SHEET

Procedure for Set C

Children are given two identical cups and are asked to put exactly the same amount of water into each cup. Then they are given an aluminum pie pan or other low-sided container. Children should pour the water from one of the cups into the pie pan. Is there more water in the cup (that still has water in it) or in the pie pan? Or is there the same amount of water in the cup and the pie pan?

Children can be encouraged to pour water back and forth from cup to pie pan to cup. However, when they make their final conclusions, they should start with the same amount of water in the two cups. They should pour the water from one of the cups into the low-sided container.

Procedure for Set D

Children receive two pieces of plasticine that are exactly the same size. The pieces are in the shape of a cube or rectangular solid.

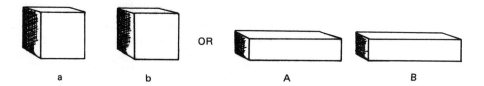

Small measuring sticks or tapes should be available for those children who know how to use them. All children should be encouraged to find a way to tell that cube (a) is the same size as cube (b), and rectangle (A) is the same size as rectangle (B).

Children should then mold each of the rectangular shaped pieces of plasticine into balls. Ask them to compare the balls. Are they the same size? Children should be asked to make sure that each ball is the same size (as the other). They then choose one of the balls and roll it out into a sausage shape. Is there more clay in the ball, is there more in the sausage, or is there the same amount in each?

Procedure for Set E

Two sets of blocks each containing twelve blocks are given to the children. The blocks in each set should be exactly the same size. Children should build one set of blocks into a skyscraper. They can build the other set into any shape they wish except a skyscraper.

After completing their buildings, the children will decide if there are more blocks in the skyscraper, more in the other building, or the same amount in each building.

Comments

Each set of materials is designed to do the same thing. Each child is asked to decide if a change in shape results in a change of amount. As much as possible, children should be asked what they believe and why. The development of higher thinking processes is based on children's abilities to separate how things are from how they look.

This activity is designed for older children in the three- to five-year-age range. Most three- to five-year-olds will not be able to separate appearance from amount.

The purpose of these activities is to introduce young children to ideas about amount and appearance. If children make an error in judgment, they should be asked to explain their answers.

QUANTIFYING 5: ARRANGING OBJECTS IN ORDER

For many children this activity is very challenging. They are asked to arrange several sets of objects in an order from largest to smallest, smoothest to roughest, or warmest to coldest. Arranging objects in this way is called *serial ordering*.

Objectives

At the end of this activity children should be able to

- Group two objects on the basis of some property, such as, this is warm and this is cold or this is rough and this is smooth.

(Some children will be able to group three or more objects in a serial order on the basis of some property.)

Materials

Each child receives

- Two pieces of sandpaper; one fine and the other coarse.
- Two pieces of material; burlap and satin.
- Two pieces of tagboard; a large square and a small square.
- A large card on which a red dot and a blue dot have been placed.
- Sandpaper sets: six pieces of sandpaper, each of a different grade.
- Material set: six small pieces of material ranging from satin and cotton to wool and burlap.
- Tagboard shape set: six squares, six circles, and six triangles in varying sizes.

Procedure

1. Distribute the sandpaper, material and tagboard pieces in separate envelopes. Ask the children to examine the materials.

2. Give each child the response card (a large card that has a red dot and a blue dot painted or drawn on it).

3. Have children place the smooth material on one dot and the rough material on the other. They can place the large shape on one dot and the small shape on the other dot.

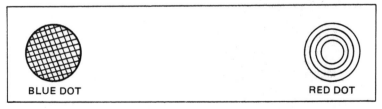

BLUE DOT   RED DOT

4. After a short period of time, distribute the sets containing large numbers of objects. Have the children arrange each set of objects in some order on the large card. The roughest piece of material can be placed on the blue dot. The smoothest can be placed on the red dot. Other pieces can be arranged in order from roughest to smoothest. This can be repeated with each set of materials.

5. Discuss with the children the ways in which they order the objects. Ask them to describe what they did and why they did it.

Comments

Many children find serial ordering to be difficult. To help children, differences in size or texture should be obvious. It might help to color code all objects in a set. That is, the largest triangle might be red, the next largest orange, and the next yellow, and so forth. In this way, children can discuss particular objects in a set using words (colors) with which they are familiar.

COMMUNICATING 1: THE PROPERTY GAME

In this activity, children are encouraged to name the properties that best describe an object.

Objectives

At the end of this activity children should be able to

- Recognize that various objects possess different properties.
- Name the following general properties and point to one object that has that property — shine, smell, texture, hardness, size, color, shape.

Materials

Each group of children receives a set of objects selected from among the following:

A bottle cap, pencil, crayon, plastic spoon, toothbrush, metal spoon, screw, sponge, rack, shell, paper clip, clear plastic such as a cup, birthday candle, clean tin can, baggie, piece of soap, band-aid, small bag of plasticine, napkin, piece of aluminum foil, golf tee, piece of satin or velveteen, small piece of wool, piece of felt, piece of sandpaper, piece of gauze, small paper bag, a marble, a picture of an elephant, and a picture of a mouse.

Procedure

1. It is suggested that children work in groups of three with a group leader for each group. Children who are able may be selected as group leader. Otherwise, an adult (teacher or aide) should serve in that capacity.

2. Explain the rules to the children. The leader begins by describing one of the objects, for example: it is (1) round, (2) hard and (3) shiny. Properties are given one at a time. What is it?

3. A child who thinks he knows what it is after the first property is given may select that object from among the others in the set. If the child is correct, he may then select another object to be described. If the child is not correct, the leader names another property and so on.

4. After naming each property, only one child is allowed to try to select the object. If no one selects the correct object, the leader tries again.

5. If a child does select the correct object, that child may then pick out the next object to be described. The child then names an accurate property of that object. If a child can name three properties and no one else in the group can identify the object the selector has in mind, that person can remain selector.

Comments

This is an activity that should be conducted as a game. Enthusiasm by the leader and relatively fast naming of properties keeps the game moving. For better cooperation, children can work in pairs, trying to select objects or name properties for the group leader to call out.

The group leader can help children with the properties they give to the group. The leader assesses who is able and who is not able to state the names of properties.

COMMUNICATING 2: THE "BLIND" TEACHER

By means of this activity children learn to describe objects and their positions to their "blind" teacher.

Objectives

At the end of this activity children should be able to

- Describe characteristics of some common objects.
- Describe the position of recognizable objects.

Materials

Each group of children receives

- Twenty construction paper circles in 5 colors.
- Twenty construction paper squares in 5 colors.
- Eighteen combinations of circles and squares in 3 colors.
- Photographs of each child in the class.
- Felt board or similar mounting surface.
- Master set of colors and shapes.

Procedure

1. Explain to the children that their teacher is a "blind" teacher. Someone has placed some shapes on a board and the shapes must be removed one at a time.

2. Ask for a helper. The helper's job consists of holding up a color selected from the master set so that others in the group can see the color. Someone in the group must then name the color and verbally lead the "blind" teacher to select a circle in that color and remove it from the board. Thus, the children have to help the teacher move up, down, left, right, above, or below, to pick the appropriate circle.

3. In a similar way, squares and combinations of squares may be used. Pictures of children in the class can be mounted on a piece of tagboard or on a felt board. Children can help the "blind" teacher find pictures on the board and remove them.

Comments

This activity can be conducted with a small group of children or with the entire class. Small groups may encourage more participation of individual children.

COMMUNICATING 3: THINGS WE CAN HEAR BUT CANNOT SEE

This activity is designed to encourage children to describe properties of objects that can be heard but cannot be seen.

Objectives

At the end of this activity children should be able to

- Describe at least one property of an unseen object.
- Give one reason why the unseen object has that property.

Materials

- Fifty baby food jars with lids — 5 sets of 10 each.
- Marble, jingle bell, stone, paper clip, a screw, a penny, rice, popcorn, sand, and plasticine.
- Paint for jars.

Procedure

1. Children should work on this activity alone. The baby food jars can be covered with aluminum foil or clouded by latex or enamel paint so that they are opaque (See comments).
2. Code each of the jars in some way (color code or use a letter for each). Ask each child to find out (a) one property of the object and (b) if possible, what is in each jar without opening the jar.
3. Discuss with the children what property and what object they think is in their jar and above all why they think so.

Comments

Each child does not have to be evaluated. Instead, they can communicate with each other about what they think is in each jar and why. Perhaps after working awhile individually, some children might benefit from sharing their observations with others.

Paint the jars by placing latex or enamel inside the jar, capping the jar tightly and shaking vigorously. The jar becomes coated with paint. Uncap immediately so the top doesn't become permanently affixed to the jar.

COMMUNICATING 4: NAME THE SPEAKER

As a result of this activity children should be able to recognize their own tape-recorded voices and identify sounds communicated on a tape recorder.

Objectives

At the end of this activity children should be able to

- Identify their voices on a tape recording.
- Identify the source of a sound recorded and played back for them.

Materials

The materials needed are

- A tape recorder and audio tape.
- Objects around the classroom such as pencil sharpener, desk drawer, windows, doors, and so on.

Procedure

1. Begin by taping children's voices in groups of four to six per segment. Have children speak in their normal voices for about ten to thirty seconds. Advance the tape so that a blank space of about thirty seconds of recording exists after each child's voice.

2. After recording the various voices and at a time when children are not present, record a sound after each child's voice. For example, after the first child's voice, record the sound of a pencil being sharpened.

3. After the second child's voice, record the sound of a door opening and closing and so on. Allow several weeks to pass. Get the children together who have had their voices recorded on a particular segment of tape and play back the recording.

4. All of the children should recognize their own voices when they hear them. Then, each child repeats the second sound by acting out in the class what was heard on the tape. Only the person whose voice has been recorded may identify and act out the second sound. (For example, child one would sharpen a pencil.)

Comments

The teacher keeps a record of who and what sounds have been recorded. If the recorder has a counter, use it to keep track of voices and associated sounds.

Some sounds that can be used are opening and closing a jar; moving a chair and/or table; opening a window; pulling up a shade; opening and closing a drawer; dropping a block of wood; or writing on the chalkboard.

COMMUNICATING 5: I CAN'T HEAR YOU!

This activity is based on the game of charades. Children are given taped messages which they must transmit to other children without speaking.

Objectives

At the end of this activity children should be able to

- Communicate a word or phrase to other children without stating the word aloud.
- Demonstrate that communicating is a way of sending messages from one person to another.
- Show that there are many ways in which people can communicate.

Materials

Since this is a group activity, the materials needed are

- A tape recorder.
- A tape with recorded messages.
- A timer or stop watch.
- A chalkboard and chalk.

Procedure

1. The children should be divided into two groups. Each group sits on the floor on opposite sides of the classroom. Before starting this activity the teacher tape records a series of words or phrases on a cassette tape. The tape recorder with earphones (so only one child can hear the message) is placed in the center of the classroom.

2. A child from one of the groups is chosen and listens to the word or phrase (using the earphones). Each word is given once and then repeated once.

3. The child must then give the message to the group without saying the word aloud or mouthing the word. The child can point to objects, act out the word, or do anything other than speak, mouth, or write the word.

4. If a member of a group can repeat the word or phrase within thirty seconds, the team earns five points. If the word is communicated within two minutes, the team earns two points. After two minutes, the player and team are out.

5. A member from the other team is then chosen to listen to the next taped word or phrase and communicate the message to that team. The score is recorded and the game ·can go on as long as interest lasts.

6. Suggested words or messages include: I like you; play with me; American flag; truck; house; grocery store; tree; green; the doll is sick.

7. After the game, the group should discuss some of the problems they met in playing the game. A very short discussion about the meaning of communication could be carried out. Children should become aware that messages are sent by the process called communication. They should begin to recognize the need for accurate communication if they hope to get their message to someone.

Comments

When taping the messages for the children to transmit, be sure to leave blank tape between words. Children should hear the word or phrase twice and then turn off the tape recorder.

DESCRIBING PROPERTIES 1: COMPARISONS

In this activity children are encouraged to observe solid objects and develop a vocabulary useful in describing the properties of those objects. Efforts are focused on terms that describe opposing properties such as rough and smooth, or tall and short, etc.

Objectives

At the end of this activity children should be able to

- Name the following properties: rough/smooth; heavy/light; tall/short; wide/narrow; shiny/dull; and hard/soft.
- Point to an object possessing one of the above properties.

Materials

Each child receives the following two-member sets:

- A piece of paper and an equal-size piece of sandpaper.
- A rock and a feather.
- A dowel 10 inches long and a dowel 2 inches long.
- Pictures or sketches showing (a) a wide avenue and a narrow alley; (b) a wide building next to a narrow building; (c) a wide automobile next to a narrow automobile.
- A piece of (dull) bond paper and an equal-size piece of aluminum foil.
- A metal washer and a cotton ball.
- A tray.
- Six objects which possess one of the properties of each of the first 6 sets above.

Procedure

1. Distribute all of the materials. Each set of opposites should be in a separate bag. Do not give any directions. Allow the children to look through their objects and play with them.
2. After a period of time, tell the children to place all of the objects into the various bags they came in.
3. Tell the children each bag contained two objects and the objects were placed together for a very important reason.
4. Let children work together to get things back in their original bags. Try to get children to see that objects in each bag had contrasting properties. Discuss these, naming each property. It may be necessary to tell children which objects go together in a bag.
5. Distribute objects which possess one of the properties of each of the original sets (for example, either rough or smooth, long or short, etc). Have children place objects into the appropriate bags. Check the children's work and discuss what they have done with the objects.

Comments

A scavenger activity might be included. Give children enough time to make decisions.

DESCRIBING PROPERTIES 2: MORE COMPARISONS

In this activity children are encouraged to observe liquid and gaseous materials and to develop a vocabulary useful in describing the properties of liquids and gases. Tests such as hot and cold, odor and odorless, thick and runny, colored and colorless are stressed.

Objectives

At the end of this activity children should be able to

- Name the following properties: hot and cold, odor and odorless, thick and runny, colored and colorless.

- Point to an object possessing one of the above properties.

Materials

Each group of children receives

- A basin of warm water and a basin of cold water.

- A pill bottle containing inexpensive perfume.

- A baggie containing air and a baggie into which a few droplets of perfume have been placed.

- A baggie of air collected above a burning candle or can of sterno and a baggie of air collected out-of-doors (if it is cold) or from inside a refrigerator.

- A small vial of baby oil, glycerin and a vial of water.

- A small vial of water laced with food coloring and a vial of clear water.

- A closed jar containing a few pieces of solid iodine and a hot plate.

Procedure

One adult works with each small group of children, doing the following:

1. Ask the children to tell one thing about each member of each set of materials to be shown (demonstrated).

2. Let the children examine several sets themselves. Demonstrate the other sets with the children.

3. What can they tell about the members of each set? Work on the vocabulary using terms the children understand. It may be useful to tape record the children's feedback.

4. Using the original materials, name a property and have the children point to an object or objects that possess the property. Encourage the children to search through the room and/or the outdoor play area to find other things that have the properties under consideration.

Comments

This activity is useful in developing children's observational and communication skills.

DESCRIBING PROPERTIES 3: SORTING BY PROPERTIES

In this activity children sort sets of objects on the basis of a single property. Then, with some help from the teacher (if needed), they sort a few objects using a second property.

Objectives

At the end of this activity children should be able to

- Sort a set of objects on the basis of a single property such as color, shape, or texture.
- Name the property used to sort the objects.

Materials

Each child receives a bag containing

- A red plastic spoon.
- A wooden coffee stirrer.
- A toothpick.
- A red balloon.
- A red crayon.
- A wooden dowel.
- A red rubber band.
- A red button.
- A 3x5 index card.
- A red pencil.
- A red piece of cellophane.

Each child later receives a bag containing

- 4 triangles (red, blue, green, yellow); 3 squares (red, blue, green); 3 rectangles (blue, green, yellow); all made of paper.
- 2 triangles, 2 squares, 1 rectangle; all cut from sandpaper.

Procedure

1. Distribute the first set of materials. Let the children spread out their materials and observe the objects in any way they choose.

2. Children may begin sorting the objects on their own. If not, after a period of time, suggest that each child sort the objects on the basis of some property. If possible, the child may want to sort the same objects using other properties.

3. Distribute the other set of materials. Ask the children to sort these objects according to shapes. After they have sorted the objects in this way, ask them if they could divide each grouping again according to some other property.

Comments

This activity can also be used to help children understand the process of classifying. For children who are successful at classifying, this activity is a good reinforcement.

DESCRIBING PROPERTIES 4: COUNTING SETS OF OBJECTS

In this activity children sort a set of objects on the basis of one given property, then count the number of objects in each grouping to determine the number of objects in each subset.

Objectives

At the end of this activity children should be able to

- Sort a set of buttons on the basis of color.
- Count the number of buttons in each subset and state that number.
- Select the numeral that represents the number of buttons in each subset.

Materials

Each child receives

- A set of 12 buttons (in five colors).
- A tray.
- A set of numerals from one to five, each numeral written on a separate 3x5 index card.

Procedure

1. Distribute a tray and a package of twelve buttons. The buttons should be in five colors and no more than five of one color.
2. Ask the children to sort the buttons.
3. After the children have sorted their buttons (most, if not all, will sort on the basis of color), give them a set of numerals, two each of numerals one to five (on index cards). Ask them to count the buttons in each subset they have made and place the buttons on the correct numeral. They can put the extra numerals aside.
4. Check with individuals to see if they can name the numeral and relate it to a set of objects of that number.

Comments

Children may choose a property other than color for classifying their buttons. This is acceptable as long as they can name the property they used.

DESCRIBING PROPERTIES 5: DESCRIBING THIS AND THAT

Using materials from the two previous activities and a screen or shadow box, children attempt to describe properties of objects they cannot see directly.

Objectives

At the end of this activity children should be able to

- Describe properties of objects that are not observed directly.
- Recognize that some properties are more easily described than others.

Materials

Each group of children receives

- Selected materials from two preceding lessons.
- A shadow box or screen with light sources.

Procedure

1. Show the children the silhouettes of several objects they have previously observed. Have the children identify the objects.
2. Then ask the children to describe as many properties of each object as they can and to defend their statements. Make sure that children are aware that they are not directly observing the properties they name.
3. Show them the objects and let them name additional properties if they can.

Comments

The screen or shadow box used in Observing 14 can be used for this activity. The number of children who participate in this activity may be small. Do not force children to take part in any sciencing activity.

Children can hold up objects for other children to observe, too. They can actually help each other develop a vocabulary needed for describing objects.

PROPERTIES OF SOLIDS, LIQUIDS, AND GASES 1: A LOOK AT SOME SOLIDS

Children observe many solid objects in this activity. They will try to find out how solids are alike. They are encouraged to pay particular attention to the shapes of solids.

Objectives

At the end of this activity children should be able to

- Identify objects as being solids.
- Recognize the shapes of solid objects.

Materials

Each child receives the following sets of objects:

- Set 1: button, shell, piece of wood, paper clip, plastic spoon, washer, small tile.
- Set 2: cotton ball, piece of yarn, swatch of material, piece of paper toweling, small sample of carpeting.
- Set 3: piece of cardboard, small pencil, a pebble or rock, piece of sponge, small piece of styrofoam, a sugar cube.

Procedure

1. Distribute a set of objects to each child and encourage the child to study the objects. When the child knows how the objects are alike, the child whispers this to the teacher.

2. Next, distribute the second set, then the third set. The children should be aware that all the objects are solids.

3. Tell the children that all the objects in this activity are called solids. How are they alike? How are they different?

Comments

Do not spend time coaxing responses from all the children. If they tire of a set but cannot tell anything about it, give them a new set. Some children understand much more than they are able to discuss. Do not push the children for verbal responses.

PROPERTIES OF SOLIDS, LIQUIDS, AND GASES 2: MIX 'N MATCH

In this activity children mix a number of liquids and discover that some mix together very nicely and others do not mix at all.

Objectives

At the end of this activity children should be able to

- Identify the materials being mixed in this activity as liquids.

- Show that some liquids mix and some do not.

Materials

Each child receives

- Five plastic dropper bottles. Each bottle contains one of five liquids: water, baby oil, after shave lotion, liquid starch, grape or lemon juice.

- Waxed paper.

- Stirrer.

- Eye dropper.

Procedure

1. Distribute the materials to each child.

2. Cover tables with newspapers and have the children wear smocks.

3. Encourage the children to mix the various liquids to see what happens to each combination. Discuss what happens with individual children.

4. Children should realize that all the materials being investigated are liquids.

5. Ask the children if all liquids mix in the same way — why or why not?

Comments

At this time, return to some of the solid objects and have the children think about how the liquids are different from the solids as well as how the liquids are different from one another.

This activity is likely to be messy. Be prepared. Children may wish to draw liquids from the pill bottles using eye droppers. Help the children learn how to use the droppers.

PROPERTIES OF SOLIDS, LIQUIDS, AND GASES 3: FIZZ—BANG!

This activity consists of a short demonstration of matter changing rapidly from a solid to a liquid to a gas.

Objectives

At the end of this demonstration children should be able to

- Describe how a solid powder was changed when it was mixed with a liquid and that the change caused bubbles and foam to form.
- Explain that after the solid changed, the cork blew out of the tube.

Materials

The materials to be used are

- One large test tube.
- Baking soda/sodium bicarbonate.
- Vinegar.
- One cork — that just fits the test tube rather tightly.

Procedure

1. Place about 1 tablespoon of baking soda powder on a circular piece of darkly colored construction paper. Let the children study this powder and describe it to one another. Is it a solid?

2. Then place the powder into the test tube. Put the cork in the end of the test tube and shake the tube well. What happened? (Nothing.)

3. Carefully add enough vinegar to cover the baking powder. Cork this mixture immediately. Shake the test tube. As the pressure of the expanding carbon dioxide in the test tube builds, the cork will finally blow off the tube.

4. By varying the amounts of the materials used, the vigor of the explosion can be varied. Do not dwell on the concept of gas at this time but do not discourage children from finding out that bubbles in a liquid indicate the presence of a gas.

Comments

Make sure that children stand well back from the demonstration. Be careful not to point the cork at the children.

PROPERTIES OF SOLIDS, LIQUIDS, AND GASES 4: THE CANDY MAKER

The intent of this activity is to provide an opportunity for children to observe changes in physical state as a solid (sugar) dissolves in water and then recrystallizes as rock candy. Some children may realize that the rock candy and the original sugar are the same material.

Objectives

At the end of this activity children should be able to

- Describe how the sugar disappeared in the water — but was still there.
- Identify sugar as a solid.

Materials

The group requires

- A sauce pan.
- Stove or hotplate.
- 1 lb. granulated sugar.
- Stirrer (spoon or glass rod).

Each child should have

- A 2-5 oz. plastic cup.
- String tied to a pencil or long nail.

Procedure

1. As a group demonstration, place cold water in a sauce pan and allow 3 or 4 children to taste the water.
2. Ask them to describe the taste.
3. Then using a hotplate, bring the water to a boil. Reduce the heat, add sugar to the hot water and stir.
4. Add sugar until no more will dissolve. Allow the mixture to cool and pour into individual plastic cups.
5. Ask children to taste this (sugar) water. Using a string tied firmly to a pencil or other stick, place the stick across the mouth of the cup, letting the string extend well into the liquid.
6. Set the cup aside for several days. Crystals of rock candy will begin to form along the string.

Comments

A small weight such as a thumbtack or paper clip can be attached to the free end of the string to act as an anchor to hold the string fairly taut in the cup of liquid.

The rock candy can be crushed using a pestle and mortar. The crystals formed can be compared to the original sugar crystals. They are identical. If children are to eat any of the rock candy, make sure all materials used in the preparation are clean.

PROPERTIES OF SOLIDS, LIQUIDS, AND GASES 5: SHELLS AND MORE SHELLS

This activity is designed to provide children with an opportunity to sort sea shells.

Objectives

At the end of this activity children should be able to

- Sort a set of sea shells according to some self-selected observable property.
- Identify sea shells as solid objects.

Materials

Each child receives

- A set of 15 sea shells of various shapes and sizes in a container.
- An egg carton — for sorting.

Procedure

1. Distribute shell sets and egg cartons to the children. Let the children study, manipulate, and possibly sort the shells without directions.
2. After an appropriate period of time, ask the children to sort the shells.
3. Ask them how and why they arranged the shells as they did.

Comments

Remember, when children sort objects, they should be encouraged to decide on the observable properties they intend to use. Do not tell them which properties to use.

PROPERTIES OF SOLIDS, LIQUIDS, AND GASES 6: THE SHAPE OF THINGS

In this activity children observe the effect of temperature on the rate at which food coloring diffuses in water. In addition, children should observe that as colored water is poured from a container of one shape into a container of a different shape the liquid takes the shape of its container.

Objectives

At the end of this activity children should be able to

- Identify warm and cold water by observing the rate of mixing of food coloring in the water.
- Describe how the colored water takes the shape of the container into which it is placed.

Materials

Each group of children receives

- Four cups of water: one very warm, one lukewarm, one cool, one ice cold.
- Food coloring.
- Glass containers of four or five different shapes.

Procedure

1. In a group demonstration, pour water into four large containers. The water in container A should be very warm (heated); the water in container B should be lukewarm; the water in container C should be cool; and the water in container D should have been chilled with ice cubes.
2. Have the children observe the containers and determine how they are different from one another.
3. Then add food coloring to each cup. Do not stir.
4. Ask children to observe what happens.
5. Add a second color to each container and observe what happens.
6. Take two cups of water and tell the children that one contains very cold water and one contains very warm water.
7. Ask the children to find out which is hot and which is cold without touching the water. Try out children's suggestions.
8. Using glass containers of a variety of shapes (but all of about the same volume), pour some colored water into one of them. What is the shape of the water?
9. Then pour the water into each of the other containers. Does the liquid seem to take a different shape as it is poured into each of the containers?

Comments

This is mainly a teacher demonstration activity with some children participating. It may be best to carry out this activity several times, dividing the group into a number of smaller groups so that each child is very near where the action is taking place. Be careful when working with hot water if children are nearby. Glass containers in the shape of various fish, birds, small animals, tall and thin or wide and flat can be used to demonstrate that water takes the shape of the container into which it is poured.

PROPERTIES OF SOLIDS, LIQUIDS, AND GASES 7: TELLING ABOUT AIR

This activity is designed to encourage children to describe properties of air. Children will demonstrate properties to other children with the help of their teacher.

Objectives

At the end of this activity children should be able to

- Tell that air is all around.
- Tell that an empty cup is really a cup full of air.
- Show how air pushes on things.

Materials

Each group needs

- Four large balloons.
- Two plastic beakers and two straws.
- One football inflator.
- One balloon air pump.
- Two syringes connected by plastic tubing.
- 4 x 6 index cards – 1 per child.
- A one-gallon plastic aquarium or plastic shoe box and some paper toweling.

Each child needs

- One plastic cup.
- One 4 x 6 index card.

Procedure

1. Tell the children that some people think that air is everywhere. Ask them what they think.

2. Lead into a series of demonstrations in which the children have been coached in advance and prepared to present the following demonstrations (one per child):

   a. Blow up a balloon. Touch it, squeeze it, and push on it. Let the air escape while squeezing the nozzle. Air can be heard, too.

   b. A cup full of water and a straw are needed. The demonstrator must do what the children in the class suggest to empty the cup. However, the cup cannot be touched in any way and lips cannot touch the straw. Can they get the water out of the cup?

   c. Place dry paper toweling into a cup so that the towel is completely inside the cup. A one-gallon aquarium about 2/3 full of water is then introduced. The cup is placed upside down into the aquarium and held under water a minute. Ask the children if they are sure the paper is completely soaked. Then remove the cup and let the children touch the paper. It is still dry. Be certain that the cup is not tilted as it is plunged into the water.

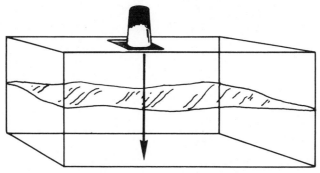

d. Fill a cup with water. Place a 4 x 6 index card over the lip of the cup. Holding the card tightly to the cup, invert the entire cup/paper system and carefully remove the hand that was holding the card. The card should not fall from the lip of the cup and no water should spill.

Caution: Do this demonstration over a sink or a bowl. Sometimes the card falls too soon and the water spills out.

Distribute cups and cards to interested children. Ask them to try this themselves and find out why the card does not fall.

e. Connect two plastic syringes with a piece of plastic tubing. Push in on the plunger of one syringe. What happens to the plunger of the other? Allow the children to investigate this syringe system. Check with individual children to see if they can relate the various demonstrations to the statement that air is all around. Can they tell anything else about the properties of air from the demonstrations?

Comments

In this series of activities it is important to let the children help with the demonstrations and to test what they have seen. These activities may take several days to complete. If children lose interest, do not force them to continue their involvement.

PROPERTIES OF SOLIDS, LIQUIDS, AND GASES 8: DISAPPEARING LIQUIDS

In this activity children observe the phenomenon of evaporation.

Objectives

At the end of this activity children should be able to

- Recognize that water has disappeared from a container or surface.
- Tell that the water has gone into the air.

Materials

- A chalkboard.
- Two wet sponges.
- A fan or other device to create a fanning effect.

Each child needs

- A plastic cup.
- One eyedropper.
- One china marker.

Procedure

1. Ask two volunteers to assist in a demonstration. Have each child wet a section of the chalkboard using a sponge.
2. Then direct the breeze from a fan (or paper fan) on the section of the board that was moistened. The other part of the board should not be fanned in any way.
3. Ask the children to observe what happens. Where did the water go?
4. Distribute a plastic cup and china marker to each child. Have the children fill their cups about half full and mark the level of the water using their china markers.
5. Also have the children place a secret mark on their cups so that they will recognize them later.
6. Have the children check the water level every day for a week or until the water has evaporated entirely. Where did the water go?

Comments

During the winter months when the humidity in most classrooms is extremely low, the water evaporates quite rapidly. At other times of the year, evaporation proceeds very slowly.

This activity is designed to allow children to observe changes in form and shape using their eyes and their sense of taste.

Objectives

At the end of this activity children should be able to

- Demonstrate that jello changes form when it cools.
- Show that jello can take many shapes when it is hot and wet (liquid) but forms one shape once it has set.

Materials

Each small group of children needs

- One small packet of flavored gelatin mix.
- One cup of hot water.
- One-half tray of ice cubes.
- One bowl.
- Spoons for each child.
- A small mold for each child.

Procedure

1. Allow children to taste a small amount of flavored jello.
2. Empty the packet of gelatin into a bowl and add the hot water. Follow directions on the package using the quick-set method.
3. Encourage children to make continuous observations as the gelatin dissolves in hot water and sets in the mold. Make one extra mold and allow it to stand in a very warm place so it will not set.
4. Children can then compare their set molds with the gelatin as it was at the start. What do the children observe?

Comments

Small individual molds can be made from plastic margarine tubs, obtained from stores or brought from home by the children. This activity could be used for the study of solids and liquids or could be repeated with some variations when solids and liquids are studied.

PROPERTIES OF SOLIDS, LIQUIDS, AND GASES 10: MYSTERY BOXES

In this activity children observe solids and liquids using only the sense of touch. They investigate the contents of small mystery boxes that are paired — one of which contains a solid material and the other a liquid.

Objectives

At the end of this activity children should be able to

- Tell that some objects are solid and some are liquid.

- Identify that liquids feel wet to the touch.

- Tell that some solids are hard and some are soft.

Materials

Each group of children receives

- Six small mystery boxes. The boxes must be carefully selected so that the cup just barely fits into the box. Thus, the cup cannot be easily tipped and the liquid spilled as children touch the liquid. The boxes should be paired and each pair of boxes covered with identical contact paper so that children can tell the pairs apart. A hole large enough for a child to place one finger should be cut in one side of each box.

- Box pair 1: One box has a small wooden cube; the other contains water in a cup. (Note: the box that is to contain the cup of liquid should be lined with several layers of water resistant material.)

- Box pair 2: One box contains a small stone; the other box contains a cup of baby oil.

- Box pair 3: One box contains a small piece of dry sponge; the other box contains a cup of diluted rubbing alcohol (mix the alcohol with water in a ratio of 1/3 alcohol to 2/3 water).

Procedure

1. Tell children the following: each mystery box contains something different; the boxes are in pairs; and each pair of boxes is like each other pair in some way.

2. The children try to find out how the boxes are alike by putting only one index finger through the hole in the box.

3. If a child thinks he knows how the boxes are alike, he should whisper the answer to the teacher. If the answer is accurate, ask him to see if he can find out how most liquids are alike and how most solids are alike. The child can explore further to see what else can be found out about the contents of the mystery boxes.

Comments

This may be a difficult activity for some young children. Hints may be necessary. Extra mystery boxes can be prepared so that children can confirm their observations. Soapy water, citric acid mixed with water and a small amount of vinegar, diluted citrus fruit drinks, glycerin, and oil can be used as other liquids. Shells, sawdust, a small piece of paper toweling, an unshelled nut, a marble, or a screw can be included among the solids. The box should be small enough so that a child can feel all around with one finger. A gift box made for small jewelry may be used. Cups for the liquid may be difficult to find. The small plastic cups used as medicine cups in hospitals are suggested for holding liquids.

SIMILARITIES AND DIFFERENCES 1: A PIRATE TREASURE HUNT

In this activity children pretend they are pirates looking for hidden treasure. They must observe and select objects that are similar to one another in some physical characteristics in order to fill their treasure chests and gain clues to the hidden treasure.

Objectives

At the end of this activity children should be able to

- Tell that some objects are alike and some are different.
- Identify objects that belong to a set using observable similarities.

Materials

Each child receives

- A pirate insignia or hat.
- A small treasure chest.
- Two objects for each treasure chest (as examples of things to look for). These objects may be buttons, leaves, rocks, shells, felt pieces in various shapes and colors, material of various textures, pictures, and sketches of objects.
- Twenty pairs of index cards (a total of forty cards). Each pair should have a sketch of the same object, for example, two cards should have sketches of red triangles, two should have sketches of green circles, and so on.
- Rewards for children — perhaps a candy treat. In addition, quantities of objects that are similar to (but not exactly like) the objects in the children's treasure chests should be set out at various locations in the area being used.

Procedure

1. Distribute pirate materials and treasure chests. Each treasure chest should contain two objects such as a blue button and a green button, a felt triangle and a felt rectangle, and so on.
2. Tell the children that they must look around the room for places where objects very much like the ones in their treasure chests can be found. They must find three more objects that are in some way similar to the two they have been given.
3. When the children have found three objects that are similar to the two in their treasure chest they must report to the teacher who discusses their findings with them. (How are the objects similar? How are they different?)
4. When they have found three objects that are similar to the original two, and have discussed them in terms of their similarities, the children are given an index card on which a sketch has been drawn.
5. They then look for a second card that has been placed somewhere in the area that has exactly the same sketch on it.

6. When they have found it, they bring it to the teacher, and tell how the two sketches are alike. The children are then given a special reward (candy or other reward).

Comments

Some preparation is needed for this activity. It may work well out-of-doors. Objects such as buttons and rocks should be set far enough apart so that children will not push and shove to get to the same location at the same time. The teacher should listen carefully to the children's reasons for thinking certain objects are similar. They may have reasons far different from those expected. Clues can be given to some children who need them. Do not intervene too quickly, however. Allow the children time to investigate on their own.

SIMILARITIES AND DIFFERENCES 2: WHICH ARE ALIKE?

Children examine sets of sealed paper bags (three bags per set), two of which contain objects that are similar, and one of which contains a very different object. Children must decide which two bags in the set contain the similar objects without opening the bags.

Objectives

At the end of this activity children should be able to

- Explain why they believe that the contents of two of three bags are similar.

- Name similar objects from clues provided by the teacher.

Materials

The group needs

- Multiple sets of sealed bags. Bags may contain small, hard objects such as stones, shells, buttons, or small pieces of wood. Bags should be blown up with air before being sealed tightly.

- Sets (pairs) of objects placed at key points in the room and inside paper bags.

Procedure

1. Allow each child to examine one or more sets of bags to determine which two of the three bags in a set contain similar objects.
2. Children can handle the bags, shake them, and smell them. They may not look into them, however.
3. Number the sets or mark them by color.
4. Have the children report which bags contain the similar objects, and how they know the objects are similar.
5. For those children who are interested, a second activity can be carried out. Describe the physical characteristics of an object. Let the children examine bags that have been set out in advance to determine which two contain the object being described or some similar object.

Comments

Some of the activities included in developing the process of inference can also be used here.

SIMILARITES AND DIFFERENCES 3: WHO MADE THAT SOUND?

In this activity children try to find out who is making a particular sound by determining similarities and differences between actual voice sounds of children they know and the tape recorded sounds.

Objectives

At the end of this activity children should be able to

- Recognize their own voices on a tape recorder.
- Identify the sounds made by two other children whom they know.

Materials

Each group of children needs

- A tape recorder and tape.
- The cardboard center roll from paper towels or bathroom tissue.
- Waxed paper or plastic wrap.
- Other means for slightly distorting one's voice such as a clean cloth or a kazoo.

Procedure

1. This activity is best conducted as a challenging game. It may be done with a small group of children (not less than four) or with a larger group.

2. Select one or two children to go into a room or somewhere where they cannot hear or see who is speaking into the microphone of a tape recorder.

3. Call on two more volunteers to disguise their voices in some way — perhaps by speaking through a megaphone or cardboard center roll; through waxed paper pressed against their lips; or in any other way they may wish.

4. Record the sounds made by these children.

5. Rewind the tape and call in the other children. They must decide who made the sounds.

6. This may be done in teams with a team getting one point or a poker chip for every correct answer. Each child or team should have equal opportunities to identify the sources of the sounds.

7. In addition, let each child repeat a simple phrase and record it. Play the recording back for the children and let them try to identify who made the sound. Point out that it is difficult to identify one's own voice.

Comments

Keep the activity moving at a reasonably brisk pace. Encourage all children to participate but do not force anyone to do so.

This activity could also be carried out using materials or objects commonly found in a child's surroundings. For example, the moving of a chair or table, the dropping of a book, a sneeze or cough, and other similar sounds can be used instead of or in addition to children's voices.

COMBINING, REARRANGING, AND DISASSOCIATING OBJECTS 1: PANCAKES PERFECT

In this activity children help make pancakes by telling the ingredients they want to add to the pancake batter in order to make a perfect pancake.

Objectives

At the end of this activity children should be able to

- Name the ingredients they added to the pancake batter.
- Identify the pancakes they made.

Materials

Each small group needs

- Prepared pancake batter.
- Ingredients to add to the batter: chopped nuts, bananas, blueberries, strawberries, chocolate chips, and so on.
- Two frying pans.
- Hot plate or stove.
- Shortening, butter, or margarine.
- Spatula (to flip pancakes).
- Eating utensils.

Procedure

1. Prepare pancake batter as children watch.

2. Ask the children to select three additional topping ingredients for their own special pancakes.

3. Place a small amount of batter into a greased frying pan.

4. Let the children add each of their chosen ingredients to the pancakes (that is, one ingredient per pancake).

5. Ask children to turn away. Then flip the pancakes into another frying pan so that the various pancakes are in a different order or arrangement.

6. Let the children return and try to identify which pancake is which as they cook.

7. After the pancakes are cooked, ask the children to confirm their identifications in some way.

8. They may then eat the pancakes.

9. Allow each child to participate in this activity. Discuss with each child what happened to the ingredients as they cooked. Did the ingredients change in number? Composition? Form? Appearance? Taste?

Comments

Encourage children to select a variety of added ingredients for their pancakes. It may be possible to work with two or three children at a time if the frying pans are large enough and the pancakes are small.

Children should gain the understanding that although some things seem to be altered in form and shape as they undergo physical changes, these things are not changed in quantity or basic composition. In other words, a cooked strawberry looks different but it is not physically different from a raw strawberry.

COMBINING, REARRANGING, AND DISASSOCIATING OBJECTS 2:
FOOD FOR THOUGHT

This activity is subdivided into several related parts. Children combine the juice of two or three common citrus fruits and observe changes in taste and appearance. The children also try to discover how and in what proportion to combine powdered sugar and milk in order to make frosting. They then combine a variety of vegetables to make a vegetable soup, trying to identify the uncooked and cooked vegetables by sight, taste, and smell. Finally, the children prepare a cocktail juice using a combination of fresh vegetables blended in a blender.

Objectives

At the end of this series of activities children should be able to

- Tell that foods change in appearance when they are mixed together.

- Identify common ingredients before and after cooking, mixing, or blending.

- Explain that sometimes foods can be mixed together and returned to the way they were originally; other times they cannot be returned to their original form.

- Tell that despite a change in color or a change in taste, the food is not lost — just made different.

Materials

Each group receives the following materials:

For fruit juice

- 1/2 orange cut in two.
- 1/2 lemon cut in two.
- 1/4 grapefruit cut in two.
- 1/2 lime cut in two (if available).
- A small pitcher.
- A stirrer.
- Some small paper cups.
- Sugar.

For frosting

- A small baggie containing powdered sugar.
- A small amount of fresh milk.
- A mixing bowl or similar container and a spoon.
- A cupcake.

For vegetable soup

- A variety of fresh vegetables, for example, potatoes, tomatoes, carrots, celery, peas, beans, cabbage, pepper, onion, parsley root, or other vegetables in season.
- Beef bouillon cubes and salt.
- Cooking pot and large spoon.
- Kitchen knife or paring knife (for teacher's use *only*).
- Hot plate.
- Water.
- Eating utensils and small bowl.

For cocktail juice

- The same vegetables used for the soup.
- Water.
- Blender.
- Knife (for teacher's use *only*).

Procedure

This series of activities can be conducted in any order. Children may work alone or in small groups. All groups can be working on just one activity at a time or each group can work on the activity of its choice.

A. Fruit juice activities

1. Each child receives a choice of fruits, 3 or 4 cups, and a stirrer.

2. Each type of fruit is given to a child in two pieces. One piece may be squeezed into a cup and set aside. The other piece can be squeezed into a second cup to be mixed with other juice.

3. Children may taste individual juices and the combinations of two or more.

4. Encourage children to consider the following questions: Can they identify the fruit by its taste? What happened to the taste when several fruits were combined? Can the combined juices be separated? Can the fruit be returned to its original form? What effect does sugar have on the taste of juices? Can the sugar be seen after it is mixed with the juice? What happens if sugar is placed directly on the unsqueezed fruit?

B. Frosting

1. Give each child the following materials: milk, powdered sugar, a container for mixing, a stirrer and an unfrosted cupcake.

2. Ask the children to combine the materials in such a way that they have a frosted cupcake.

3. Speak to individual children about how they mixed things, what they mixed, and how things changed.

4. Ask the children if the frosting could be unmixed, that is, returned to its original ingredients.

C. Vegetable soup

1. Children may prefer to work in small groups for this activity. An adult should be with each group at all times.

2. Children should select the vegetables for their soup. The teacher can dice those vegetables selected letting children examine diced pieces of each.

3. The children may compare the pieces of vegetable, taste them, smell them, and so on.

4. After retaining samples of each type of vegetable, the rest are placed into a pan of boiling water.

5. Add a bouillon cube for flavor.

6. Cook for 1/2 hour or until the vegetables are soft.

7. Add salt for additional flavor.

8. Ask the children to compare the cooked and uncooked vegetables as to taste, smell, and appearance. Also ask children to try to return cooked vegetable pieces to the way they were before cooking.

D. Cocktail juice

1. The procedure for this activity is quite similar to the one for vegetable soup. Ask children to identify various types of vegetables using diced vegetables. They may sort the vegetables if they want.

2. Then wash all the cubes and allow each group to decide which combination of vegetables they want for their cocktail juice.

3. Blend the selected cubes in water in a blender until they are thoroughly mixed. Add water if necessary to thin the mixture.

4. An alternative activity for more advanced children could be used as a follow-up. Since each group of children will probably select some unique combination of vegetables, mark each group's juice with a code letter being careful to record the vegetables used. Let volunteer tasters from other groups taste various juices and try to identify the exact combination of ingredients used. Using pictures of vegetables, children keep track of what they used in their group's juice. The tasters must name what they think is in the juice and why they think so. Discuss with children how they perceived different tastes and appearances in various juice combinations. Once the juice is made, can it be returned to its original form and/or taste?

Comments

An important objective of these activities is to make children aware of reversibility. Some things can return to their original form after they've been physically altered; others cannot. Observation skills are used in these activities, too. Ask the children for evidence for observations they make.

COMBINING, REARRANGING, AND DISASSOCIATING OBJECTS 3:
PLAY WITH CLAY

In this activity children try to find a way to match two quantities of plasticine in quantity and shape. They then rearrange and redesign each piece of clay using available materials and their own imaginations.

Objectives

At the end of this activity children should be able to

- Compare quantities by molding two pieces of clay so that they are about the same size and shape.

- Alter the shape of one or both of the pieces of clay and describe how the shapes were altered.

- Return the altered shapes to their original forms.

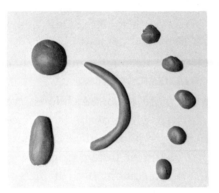

Materials

Each child receives

- Two quantities of plasticine in two colors (oil-base clay).

- A large-diameter dowel (used as a rolling pin).

- Toothpicks, marbles, small stones, and pegs.

- Cookie cutters or other forms.

The whole group needs

- An equal arm balance.

- Large supply of plasticine in the two colors.

Procedure

1. It is suggested that children work alone on this activity. Ask children to solve the following problems.

   a. Can they take two pieces of clay from the two large piles of clay so that the two pieces of clay are exactly the same size? Can they think of some way to prove that the two pieces of clay are the same size? (If they cannot do this, don't push the children).

   b. Can they then make designs, or figures, out of each piece of clay?

2. After molding the two pieces of clay, ask the children if they can make the clay look like it did at the beginning of the activity. For the purpose of molding the clay, make available to children cookie cutters or other forms, large-diameter dowels for rolling out the clay, marbles, pegs, buttons, toothpicks, stones, or anything else that might encourage children to create an interesting design.

3. If possible, discuss with individual children:

    a. How they knew that two initial quantities of clay were the same.

    b. How they rearranged their clay; what they used and what happened.

    c. How they returned the clay to its original shape and how they knew it was in its original shape.

    d. The quantities of clay in the "before" and "after" shapes of the clay.

Comments

Encourage children to be creative. Do not force them to carry out this activity. If some children merely play with the clay and are unable or unwilling to discuss their procedures, this is acceptable.

COMBINING, REARRANGING, AND DISASSOCIATING OBJECTS 4: MIXING AND UNMIXING

In this activity children observe how two substances can be mixed together, then separated using a sifter or a strainer. Children are then presented with several substances to mix and then separate. Some of the substances are easily separated while others cannot be separated as easily.

Objectives

At the end of this activity children should be able to

- Name substances and describe what happened to those substances when they were mixed.
- Demonstrate a method for physically separating rice and sugar.
- Tell why it is easier to separate some substances than it is to separate others.

Materials

- A quantity of rice; sand, and salt — each separate in a small paper cup.
- A sugar cube.
- A cup of water.
- An empty cup.
- A strainer or sifter.
- Some cheesecloth.

    For an introductory class demonstration the group leader should have

- Popcorn kernels and flour.
- A sifter or strainer.

Procedure

1. Begin with a short demonstration for the group of children involved in this activity.
2. Mix popcorn and flour thoroughly. Let the children examine the mixture.
3. Ask if anyone can suggest a simple way to separate them. Try the suggestions.
4. Have a sifter and a strainer at the location where the demonstration is taking place. Separate the substances for the children using both the strainer and the sifter.
5. Each child can choose to try challenge 1 or challenge 2. In challenge 1 each child receives a cup of water, an empty cup, some sand, a sugar cube and a piece of cheesecloth. Ask the children to mix the three, and then to find out a way to separate them. Children who choose challenge 2 receive a small cup of rice, some salt, and a sifter or fine mesh strainer. They, too, should mix their substances and then try to separate them so they return to their original forms.
6. Children may participate in both challenges if they wish. Point out that challenge 1 is more difficult than challenge 2.

Comments

Encourage children to think of creative ways to separate the substances. If no one can solve challenge 1, the teacher can show the children how in a demonstration. Mix the sand, sugar, and water. The sugar goes into the solution and the sand does not. Pour off the sugar water solution through cheesecloth into a clean cup. Let the cup stand uncovered near a window or warm area of a room for several days. The water will evaporate, leaving the sugar behind.

This activity is designed to provide additional experience with reversibility and exposure to a concept called *atomism* — the idea that materials are composed of smaller particles.

Section III Suggestions for Teachers of Young Children

INTRODUCTION

This section is designed to provide some basic information and ideas for teachers. The parts of this section include:

- Basic science information about the topics suggested for informal sciencing.
- Tips on finding, preparing, and maintaining materials and equipment.
- A list of supplies and equipment.
- Additional readings and sources of information.

BASIC SCIENCE INFORMATION FOR TEACHERS

Unit 4 of Section I deals with the meaning of informal and incidental sciencing. The same unit contains suggestions about informal and incidental sciencing activities for children. It is helpful for teachers to have some knowledge about the science concepts used for informal sciencing.

This section of the text is designed to help the reader understand some of the science concepts suggested for informal sciencing. The science information presented is very basic and should be useful for the teacher.

It is important that a teacher understand the topics and activities which will be carried out with the children. Even if children learn by their own discoveries (as they do in informal sciencing), a teacher should be aware of what the children can learn. A teacher should know whether children are reaching correct conclusions. Each topic suggested for informal sciencing is covered.

Electricity

There are two basic kinds of electricity. They are (1) current electricity (the kind that makes lights or televisions go on); and (2) static electricity (the kind that causes electrical shocks — such as when one walks across a wool carpet and then touches some metal object that is connected to the ground). For the purposes of this text, only current electricity is discussed.

Current electricity is the flow of energy from one point to another along a material that permits the flow to take place. The things that flow are tiny particles called *electrons*. Materials that carry electrons from one place to another are called *conductors*. Copper, iron, nickel, and aluminum wire are often used as conductors. In order for electrons to flow, an energy source or pusher is needed. *Generators* produce the power needed to push electrons over large distances to light houses and other buildings. On a small scale, a battery or dry cell can serve as the power source or pusher.

In order for electrons to flow, there must be a complete pathway from the power source to the user (light bulb) and back to the power source. When this path is complete,

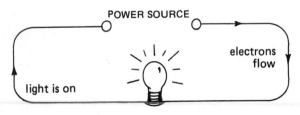

Fig. T-1. Closed circuit

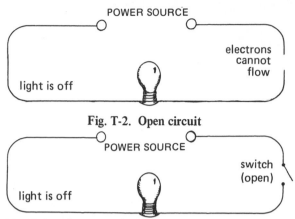

Fig. T-2. Open circuit

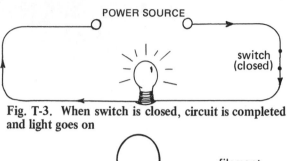

Fig. T-3. When switch is closed, circuit is completed and light goes on

Fig. T-4. When switch is open, circuit is broken and light is off

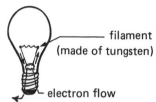

Fig. T-5. A light bulb has a complete circuit within.

the term *closed circuit* or *complete circuit* is used. See figure T-1, page 153.

If the circuit is interrupted in some way — an opening of some sort — the term *open circuit* is used. See figure T-2.

In order to control the flow of electrons in a circuit (to start or stop the flow) *switches* are used. A switch is placed somewhere along the pathway. When the switch is closed, the circuit is completed (electrons flow and lights go on). When the switch is opened, the circuit is broken (electrons cannot flow in a complete circle and lights do not go on). See figures T-3 and T-4.

As stated earlier, materials that easily allow electrons to flow from one point to another are called conductors. Some materials actually prevent electrons from flowing. These materials are called *insulators.* Rubber, glass, and procelain are examples of insulators.

When electrons flow from a power source along a conductor, heat is created. The amount of heat depends on the material of the conductor (copper, aluminum, etc.), how thick or thin it is, and the amount of power generated by the energy source. Remember, electrons must pass along a complete circuit.

If one studies a light bulb carefully, it can be seen that the light bulb is made up of a complete circuit. See figure T-5. Electrons

enter the bulb and flow up a thin post. At the top of the post the electrons travel across a thin wire *filament* made of a metal called tungsten. Electrons then flow down the post on the other side of the bulb and out through the bottom of the bulb. The flow of electrons causes the tungsten filament to become very hot. It gets so hot that it becomes white hot and glows brightly. Over time, the tungsten becomes brittle and breaks. Once the filament is broken, the circuit is broken and electrons cannot flow. Then the bulb has burned out.

The electron particles are pushed along a conductor in a very special way. This special way is related to how the pushing power is created. In a dry cell or battery, chemicals are used to create a buildup of electrons at one pole of the cell. When the buildup is great enough and a circuit is completed (from one pole of the cell through a conductor back to the other pole) electrons begin moving. An electron moves a short distance along the conductor (wire) and causes a sudden buildup of electrons at that point. The original electron or another electron may move a short distance, causing a buildup of electrons at that point. In this way, electrons flow along the conductor building up and pushing one another through the closed circuit.

Fig. T-6. A series circuit

Fig. T-7. A parallel circuit

Circuits

It is possible to study many kinds of circuits. There are two basic types:

- a *series circuit* in which electrons flow through a series of lights or other appliances before returning to the power source (see figure T-6); and

- a *parallel circuit* in which electrons flow through parallel pathways passing through one light only before returning to the power source (see figure T-7).

Figures T-8 through T-12 show five circuit arrangements that can be set up easily. Lights in a home are arranged in parallel circuits. Switches are connected to lights by means of a series circuit.

Magnetism

There are two kinds of magnets. One is found in nature and is called *lodestone*. The other is made artificially and is usually made of iron, steel, or a combination of metals. Both natural and artificial magnets work in a similar way. The large magnet is made up of small particles called *atoms*. Each atom is itself a tiny magnet. An atom has two *poles* (or charged ends). In unmagnetized materials the atoms are not arranged in any special way. That is, poles are not lined up in any order. See figure T-13, page 156.

When a material becomes magnetized, all of the atoms line up so that the poles are facing in the same directions. Poles are called either *north pole* or *south pole*. In a fully magnetized material, all north poles are lined up close to the south pole of nearby atoms.

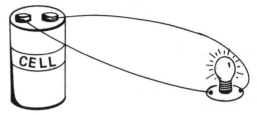

Fig. T-8. Closed circuit

Fig. T-9. Closed circuit; one light and one knife switch

Fig. T-10. Closed circuit: two lights in series and one knife switch

Fig. T-11. Closed circuit: two lights in a parallel circuit controlled by one knife switch

Fig. T-12. Closed circuits: two lights in a parallel circuit, each controlled by its own knife switch

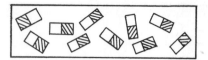

Fig. T-13. **Atoms in unmagnetized materials.**

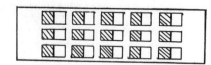

Fig. T-14. **Atoms in magnetized material**

All south poles are lined up close to the north poles of nearby atoms. See figure T-14.

If the atoms remain lined up this way for a long time (days, months, or years), the magnet is called a *permanent magnet*. If the atoms remain lined up for a short time (only when touching a permanent magnet or when connected to a source of current electricity), the magnet is said to be a *temporary magnet*.

It is possible to stroke a piece of steel such as a sewing needle and magnetize the needle. This can be done if the needle is stroked in the same direction using only one pole of a bar magnet. See figure T-15.

Magnetic attraction. Magnets attract other magnets. They also attract materials that contain iron or a combination of iron and other substances. For instance, steel is made of iron, carbon, and other materials, and is attracted by a magnet.

Magnetic attraction can pass through certain materials. For instance, a magnet can be placed on one side of a thin piece of plastic. Thumbtacks are attracted through the plastic. See figure T-16. Magnetic attraction also passes through glass, water, pure copper, paper, and wood. A thin sheet of iron, however, lessens the magnetic attraction. Much of the force of the magnet is absorbed by the iron.

Magnets also affect compasses. When a magnet is brought near a compass, the needle of the compass swings around.

Shapes of magnets. Artificial magnets come in a variety of shapes. Some are shaped like bars. The force of the magnet seems to be concentrated at either end of a bar magnet. See figure T-17.

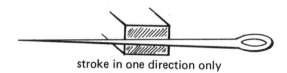

stroke in one direction only

Fig. T-15. **Magnetizing a sewing needle**

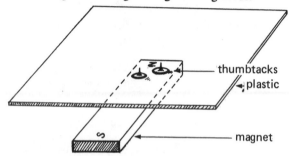

thumbtacks

plastic

magnet

Fig. T-16. **Magnetic attraction can pass through some materials.**

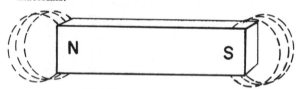

N   S

Fig. T-17. **Bar magnet**

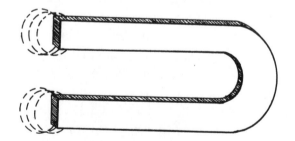

Fig. T-18. **Horseshoe magnet**

Fig. T-19. **Round magnet**

Some magnets are shaped like horse-shoes. The power of these magnets seems to be concentrated at the two open ends. See figure T-18.

Some magnets are shaped like flat doughnuts. See figure T-19.

Magnetic fields. One can study the way magnetic attraction works by using small pieces of iron called *iron filings*. The iron filings can be sprinkled on a piece of paper. Then a bar magnet is placed under the paper near the filings. The filings make a pattern as they are attracted to the magnet. Magnets obviously give off an invisible force. This force takes a special shape and is called the magnetic field. See figure T-20.

When two bar magnets are brought near each other in the presence of iron filings, the magnetic attraction of the poles can be observed. It can easily be seen that *like poles repel* (see figure T-21) and *unlike poles attract* (see figure T-22).

Floating and Sinking

Water and other liquids have the ability to hold certain objects up and keep them from sinking. Other objects sink as soon as they are placed in water.

If a cube· of solid steel is placed in water, the steel immediately sinks. If that same cube of steel is reshaped into a boat, the steel can float. In the case of the cube, the weight of the steel is distributed over a small size (volume). In the case of the boat, the same weight of steel is spread out over a much larger volume.

Objects that sink in water. When an object is placed in water it pushes the water aside. The water is said to be *displaced*. The amount of water pushed aside is related to the *volume* (length, width, and height) of the object placed in the water. If the water is in a glass or a bathtub, one can see the level of the water

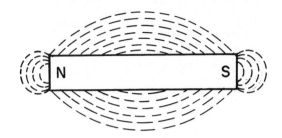

Fig. T-20. A magnetic field

Fig. T-21. Like poles repel

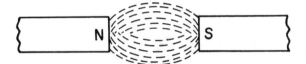

Fig. T-22. Unlike poles attract

rise as the water is displaced. In a large body of water such as a lake or swimming pool, it is more difficult to detect the rise (or displacement) of the water.

Water displacement can be observed when one sits down in a bathtub. The water is pushed aside and must go somewhere. Thus, the level of water rises.

What happens if a bathtub is filled to the top and someone sits down in it? Obviously, the bathtub would overflow. The amount (volume) of water that has overflowed is exactly equal to the volume of that much of the person that is in the water.

The amount of water that is displaced by an object placed in the water is always related to the total size (volume) of the object. The greater the volume of the object, the greater the amount of water that is displaced. The smaller the volume of the object, the smaller is the volume of water displaced.

The amount of water that is displaced does not depend on the weight of the object. It depends only on the volume.

Objects that float in water. Some objects are very heavy when the weight of the object is compared to the volume of the object. For example, a cube of lead that is one inch in length, one inch in width, and one inch in height is relatively heavy. Aluminum of the same volume is relatively light. A cube of lead is thus heavier than the same size cube of aluminum. A cube of iron is heavier than the same size cube of water. See figure T-23.

When objects are placed into a liquid, they tend to sink due to the force of their weight. However, there is a force that pushes up on objects in a liquid, too. This force that pushes up is called a *buoyant force* or *buoyancy.* The buoyant force on an object is related to the size and weight of that object.

As in the case of objects that sink in a liquid, objects that float also push aside (displace) liquid. The amount of liquid displaced is related to the volume of the object. The greater the volume of an object, the greater is the amount of liquid displaced.

If the volume of an object could be increased without changing its weight, the object might be made to float in a liquid. As the volume of an object increases, the amount of liquid that is displaced also increases. The greater the amount of liquid displaced, the greater is the buoyant force of that liquid.

Sound

Objects make noise when they move back and forth very rapidly. Back and forth movements are called *vibrations.* Only objects that are vibrating rapidly make noise. Objects that are vibrating slowly or are not vibrating at all do not make noises that the human ear can detect.

Fig. T-23. **A cube of iron is heavier than the same size cube of water.**

Sound has three qualities: (1) *pitch* — highness or lowness of sounds; (2) *loudness*; and (3) *timbre* (pronounced tamber) — the quality of a sound.

Pitch. The highness or lowness of a sound is related to the object that is vibrating. The object can be a solid, such as a string of a violin or the vocal chords in one's voice box. A column of air can also vibrate, such as the air in the pipes of an organ or the air in a tuba.

The more slowly an object vibrates, the lower the sound. An object that vibrates faster makes a higher sound.

The highness or lowness of the sound made by a vibrating string or column of air is influenced by two things: (1) how long the vibrating object is; and (2) how thick or fat it is. A long violin string vibrates more slowly than a short string. A long column of air in a pipe organ vibrates more slowly than a short column of air. Thus, a long string or long column of air produces a lower sound than a short string or short column of air. This is why putting one's finger on the strings of a violin or guitar makes the pitch higher. Putting one's finger on a string shortens the length of string that vibrates. The shorter string vibrates more rapidly and thus produces a higher sound.

A thick violin string vibrates more slowly than a thin string. Thus, a thick string makes a lower sound than a thin string. The air in a thick pipe of a pipe organ vibrates more slowly than the air in a thin pipe. Thus, a thick pipe makes a lower sound than a thin pipe.

Loudness. The harder a string is plucked or the harder a horn is blown, the louder is the sound that is made. Loudness is related to the way a string or a column of air vibrates.

If the vibrations made by the air in a horn could be seen, they might look something like figure T-24. If one were to blow very softly, the vibrations would look like figure T-25. If one were to blow very hard, the vibrations would look like figure T-26. Thus, the air inside the horn vibrates differently depending on how hard a player blows into the mouthpiece. The air around the horn also vibrates. The harder one blows, the more powerful are the vibrations in the air around the horn. In a similar way, if one taps the head of a drum very lightly, the drum makes a soft sound. If one bangs the drum head with great vigor, the drum gives off a loud sound.

Timbre. Timbre allows one to recognize the sound of an instrument. Both the violin and horn could sound a note that has the same pitch and loudness. Yet, because of the special quality (the timbre) of a violin or a horn, one can identify which note was made by which instrument. One recognizes the voice of a friend because of the timbre of the voice.

Sound travels through materials. In order for sound made by a horn or a voice to reach a person's ear, that sound must travel over a distance. The distance may be very short or quite long.

Sound is made by vibrating objects. A person's ear picks up the vibrations that reach it. That information is then sent to the brain. The brain tries to make sense out of the information.

However, in order for vibrations made by a voice to reach another person's ear, those vibrations must travel through space.

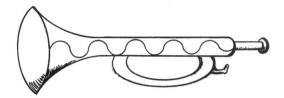

Fig. T-24. Vibrations made by air in a horn

Fig. T-25. Vibrations made when blowing softly into a horn

Fig. T-26. Vibrations made when blowing hard into a horn.

If air fills the space between one person's voice and another person's ear, the air must vibrate. If water fills the space, the water must be made to vibrate.

When a sound is made, the air next to the sound is affected. The air begins to vibrate. It pushes on the air around it, starting that air to vibrate. This goes on until the vibrating air reaches an ear. The ear contains a stretched piece of skin (like the head of a drum). This skin is called the *ear drum* and is found inside the ear. When vibrating air strikes the ear drum, the drum begins to vibrate. These vibrations are then sent as information along a nerve to a person's brain.

If there was no air between the place a sound is made and the place the sound is to be heard, there would be no sound. Vibrations must be transmitted through a substance, such as a gas (air), a liquid (water), or a solid (putting an ear up to a wall). If one could pump all the air out of a room and ring a bell in that room, a person in the next room would hear no sound.

Animals and Plants

Whether animals and plants are cared for indoors or outdoors there are certain things one should know.

Caring for animals. A rule to follow in caring for animals is this: never do anything to an animal you would not do to yourself. If this is understood, many problems can be avoided.

Humans need healthy food and clean air. They need clean surroundings, a space in which to move about, and time for sleep and rest. Animals, too, need these things.

If a human overeats and gets too fat, that person may become ill. If animals are over-fed, they become ill.

Humans need air that contains oxygen and nitrogen in order to breathe. If air is taken away, people die within seconds or minutes. If an animal is deprived of air, it will die, too. A fish also needs air. The fish, however, breathes through its gills. It takes in water and removes the oxygen from the water. If water is impure or lacks the proper amount of oxygen, fish will die.

Germs breed in dirty places. Human diseases are often picked up when a person comes in contact with bacteria or viruses. People can become sick from living among dirt and other forms of waste. Animals, too, become ill if they are not kept away from various forms of waste. They need clean surroundings, and they need to be kept clean.

Animals need ample space in which to live. When animals are confined, they may become upset. Normally, an animal has a territory — a space over which it moves about. If the territory is reduced to an unnaturally small size (as when animals are caged), the animal becomes upset. Animals in a zoo or in a classroom may develop unusual behavior patterns. This is an animal's way of adjusting to a territory that is uncomfortably small.

Animals need sleep and rest periods. They need times alone when they are not being handled. If children constantly handle an animal in their classroom or out-of-doors, they can cause unpredictable behavior in that animal.

When starting an aquarium, be certain to use aged water. Water from many city systems contains chlorine (added to the water to kill germs). As one draws water from a tap, the water may be higher than normal in chlorine content and lower in oxygen. If water is allowed to age in a container for several days, chlorine passes into the air and oxygen replaces it. Fish that are placed into water that is high in chlorine and low in oxygen may die very quickly.

Too many plants or too many fish in an aquarium can also cause problems. If there is a balance between plants and animals, the aquarium will be a clean, useful learning resource in the classroom.

Caring for plants. In order for plants to live and grow, certain basic needs must be met. Plants need light. However, most plants also need a period of darkness. Plants need water. However, plants should not be drowned. Too much water can be just as bad as no water at all. Plants need a certain amount of warmth. However, too much heat can destroy plants just as quickly as too little heat. Plants need nutritious soil in which to grow. Without traces of certain basic minerals, plants cannot grow and develop properly.

Green plants are important to human beings because they are a main source of food. Plants produce food and actually feed themselves. Animals such as cows, pigs, and sheep eat green plants. Humans then eat these animals as well as some of the plants. Green plants use sunshine, carbon dioxide (a gas found in the earth and in the air) and water to produce sugar and oxygen. People eat the sugar and breathe the oxygen. Without green plants, humans would die very quickly. The process by which plants produce food is called *photosynthesis.* Simply stated, green plants contain a green substance called *chlorophyl.* Chlorophyl has special properties. Because of chlorophyl, the energy from sunlight can be transformed into food energy for people. The energy trapped in chlorophyl is then used to convert carbon dioxide and water to a simple sugar and oxygen.

Green leaves look green because of chlorophyl. In the autumn of each year chlorophyl disappears from the leaves. Red and brown substances are also found in leaves. However, the green color of chlorophyl covers the other colors until the fall. Then when the chlorophyl is no longer present, the reds, oranges, yellows, and browns can be seen.

GATHERING AND PREPARING MATERIALS

The materials purchased for a sciencing program should be inexpensive. It is good to buy many small and less expensive materials than to buy a few large, expensive items. Science carts, expensive microscopes, and other similar items are not practical for young children and thus need not be purchased.

Plastics and Glassware

As much as possible, unbreakable materials should be used. Plastics crack and have to be thrown away. However, plastic cups are fairly inexpensive. They are not likely to shatter and cut a child's hand. However, plastics cannot be heated over an open fire. Thus, some pyrex glassware is needed. Pyrex glassware can be ordered from a science catalogue or purchased locally.

Tumblers for children to use can be found at supermarkets or other stores. They, too, are made of plastic.

Wooden Materials

There are many ways in which wood can be used in sciencing. Plywood boards into which objects can be screwed may be needed. Plywood should be sanded carefully before it is given to children. Slivers are dangerous. Wood in various textures and colors can be found in lumberyards. This wood can be cut into small pieces or ground into sawdust. Again, care must be taken to sand the wood and remove other dangerous materials (such as nails).

Metals

Manufacturing plants often throw away stampings and punch outs of many types of metals. These can be put to good use in a sciencing program. However, sharp edges and burrs must be removed. This can be done by filing, grinding or scraping.

Appliances

An electric hot plate, a blender, a tape recorder, a popcorn popper, gro-lux lights, and aquarium materials are among the electrical appliances recommended for sciencing. These are materials that should be kept by a teacher and, in many cases, used by the teacher. It is advisable to purchase high-quality items that will last a number of years.

Storage

Shoe boxes are a very convenient way to store materials. They can be brought in by teachers or purchased from manufacturers.

It is a good idea to paint the boxes. Painting can serve two purposes. First, it makes the shoe boxes more attractive. Second, the colors can serve as a code for the children. An oil base paint is best to use. Latex paints tend to spot and are easily ruined by water or moisture. A gloss or semigloss paint is bright and attractive. The shoe boxes can then be stored on low shelves and made available to children.

Larger boxes, such as soda cases or egg crates, can also be used. However, they tend to become too heavy for children to use easily. A large box (full of materials) that is dropped can also create more problems than a small box.

SUPPLIES AND EQUIPMENT

Listed on the following pages are basic supplies and equipment needed for formal and informal sciencing. It is assumed that certain basic materials are found in most classrooms and are therefore not included in these lists. (Such items are toys, blocks, doll dishes, paints, brushes, sponges, marking pencils, tagboard, construction paper, pots and pans, felt boards, crayons, shadow box, and magazines.) Each list also contains suggestions as to where materials can be most inexpensively obtained.

FORMAL SCIENCING ACTIVITIES	
Materials and Equipment	**Where to Find Them**
Aluminum trays (various sizes and shapes)	Supermarket; variety store.
Aluminum pans	Supermarket; variety store.
Aluminum pie tins	Supermarket; variety store.
Baby food jars	Ask friends to save.
Blender	Discount store; secondhand.
Buttons (wide variety)	Department store; resale shop.
Cardboard containers (for storage and as touch boxes)	Ask friends and supermarket to save; shoe store.
Cloth material (swatches or samples in various sizes, colors, and textures)	Department store; fabric store; resale shop; furniture store (carpet samples and drapery samples); ask friends for clothing discards.
Egg cartons	Ask friends to save.
Eyedroppers	Drugstore; science supply catalogue.
Food coloring	Supermarket; variety store.
Flannel board	Variety store; educational supply catalogue.
Flavor extracts	Supermarket.
Football inflator	Department store; athletic supply store.
Hot plate	Department store; resale shop.
Leaves (variety)	Gather during growing season and in fall. Mount on cardboard covered with plastic wrap.
Liquids: mineral oil, cooking oil, fruit juices, vinegar, salty water.	Supermarket; drugstore; volunteers from children's homes.
Magnifyers	Variety store; stamp collector supply store; science supply catalogue.
Musical instruments (variety)	Resale shop; auction; music store; donations.
Orange juice cans (small)	Ask friends to save.
Paint chip cards	Department store; paint supply store.
Pill bottles (small empty bottles with screw tops)	Drugstore; hospital; nursing home; science supply catalogue.
Pipe cleaners	Tobacco store; variety stores.
Plastic: cups, jars, bottles, syringes, tubes, spoons, shoe containers or one gallon aquariums.	Grocery; restaurant discards (large plastic mayonnaise jar); hospital; nursing home; science supply catalogue.
Plasticine (clay)	Variety store; hobby shop.
Plywood (1/4" or 3/8")	Ask friends; lumberyard.
Popcorn popper	Department store; resale shop.
Rocks (variety of small specimens)	Ask friends.
Sandpaper (variety of grades)	Department store; hardware store.
Shells (variety)	Ask friends; science supply catalogue.
Straws	Supermarket.
Tape recorder and audio tapes (cassette is best)	Department store; electronic supply store; resale shops.
Tools (small; variety such as a hammer, saw, etc.)	Hardware store.
Trays: meat or bakery	Ask at meat or bakery counter of a supermarket.
Wood: coffee stirrers; variety of pieces	Department store; supermarket; lumberyard.

INFORMAL SCIENCING ACTIVITIES	
Materials	**Where to Find Them**
Electrical Equipment C or D cell batteries and battery holders	Electronic supply store; drugstore; supermarket; science supply catalogue; hardware store.
Wire and wire cutters (17- or 18-gauge wire)	Hardware store; electronic supply store; science supply catalogue.
Fahnstock clips; alligator clips	Same as above.
Bulbs and sockets (metal or porcelain)	Same as above.
Switches; single pole, single throw knife switch	Same as above.
Magnetism materials Assorted magnets — horseshoe shaped; bar magnets; circular magnets	Hardware store; science supply catalogue; variety store.
Iron filings	Industrial waste; science supply catalogue; hobby shop.
Magnetic compasses	Department store; variety store; science supply catalogue.
Floating and Sinking Baby food jars with tight fitting caps, sand or gravel	Ask friends to save.
Aluminum foil	See Formal Sciencing.
Plasticine	Same as above.
Corks and rubber stoppers	Science supply catalogue.
Plastic containers; shoe boxes; aquarium; large freezer container	Department store; variety store; science supply catalogue.
Sound Soft drink bottles	Save these; ask friends to save.
Cigar boxes	Ask friends; ask druggist to save; tobacco shop.
Rubber bands of various sizes	Department store; business supply store.
Wires of various lengths and sizes	Telephone company; manufacturing discards; musical instrument store.
Old toothbrushes (as bows); pencil covered with sandpaper or stiff felt (as a bow)	Ask friends.
Comb and wax paper (a kazoo)	Local supplier.
Tin cans of various sizes; oatmeal boxes; other containers that make sounds	Ask friends; save at home.
Old musical instruments (may be partially broken); bells	Sales at music store; secondhand or resale shop; auctions.
Old silverware	Ask friends. (continued)

Materials	Where to Find Them
Tape recorders, tape players, tapes, phonographs and records	School supplier; discount store; resale shop; auction.
Living things (indoors and out) Flat or plastic containers (for growing plants)	Save at home; garden supply shop; greenhouse grower or supplier.
Soil and vermiculite for potting and growing	Greenhouse; garden supply store.
Gro-lux lights	Department store; pet shop; science supply catalogue.
Small greenhouse for classroom	Science supply catalogue.
Assorted seeds	Garden supply shop; farm supply store.
Cages, aquariums, terrariums	Pet supply store; science supply catalogue.
Birdfeeders (can be homemade or purchased)	Same as above.
Living things: gerbils; guinea pigs; small mice; goldfish; guppies; aquatic plants; salamanders; frogs; assorted plants	Same as above.

SUGGESTED READINGS

This final section contains sources of additional information for the readers. Some of the sources supply information about children, but most deal with science and science methods.

ADDITIONAL READINGS ABOUT CHILDREN

1. Baker, K.R. *Ideas that Work Withth Young Children.* Washington: NAEYC, 1972.
2. Brearly, M. and Hitchfield, E. *A Guide to Reading Piaget.* New York: Schocken Books, 1966.
3. Brophy, J. and others. *Teaching in the Preschool.* New York: Harper and Row, 1975.
4. Getzels, J. and Jackson, P. *Creativity and Intelligence.* New York: John Wiley and Sons, 1962.
5. Ginoth, H. *Teacher and Child.* New York: Macmillan Company, 1972.
6. Hess, R. and Bear, R. *Early Education.* Chicago: Aldine Publishing Co., 1968.
7. Hess, R. and Croft, D. *Teachers of Young Children.* Boston: Houghton-Mifflin, 1972.
8. Hildebrand, V. *Guiding Young Children.* New York: Macmillan, 1975.
9. Hymes, J. *Teaching the Child Under Six.* Columbus, Ohio: Chas. Merrill, 1974.
10. Krown, S. *Threes and Fours Go to School.* Englewood Cliffs, New Jersey: Prentice-Hall, 1974.
11. Lavatelli, C.S. *Piaget's Theory Applied to An Early Childhood Curriculum.* Boston: American Science and Engineering, Inc., 1970.
12. Leeper, S.H. *Good Schools for Young Children.* New York: Macmillan Co., 1968.
13. Mills, B. *Understanding the Young Child and His Curriculum.* New York: Macmillan Co., 1972.
14. Parker, R. *The Preschool in Action.* Boston: Allyn & Bacon, 1972.
15. Read, K. *The Nursery School.* Philadelphia: W.B. Saunders Co., 1971.
16. Spodek, B. *Teaching in the Early Years.* Englewood Cliffs, New Jersey: Prentice-Hall, 1972.

ADDITIONAL READINGS ABOUT SCIENCE

Science Methods and Activities

1. Blough, G. and others. *Elementary School Science and How to Teach It.* New York: Holt, Rinehart and Winston, 1974.
2. Hone, E. and others. *A Sourcebook for Elementary Science.* New York: Harcourt, Brace, Jovanovich, 1971.
3. Morholt, E. and others. *A Sourcebook for the Biological Sciences.* New York: Harcourt, Brace, Jovanovich, 1966.
4. UNESCO. *Seven Hundred Science Experiments for Everyone.* New York: Doubleday, 1962.
5. Victor, E. *Science for the Elementary School.* New York: Macmillan Co., 1970.

Science Content (Science Information for Teachers)

1. Blanc, S. and others. *Modern Science: Matter, Energy, and Space.* New York: Holt, Rinehart, and Winston, 1971.
2. BSCS. *High School Biology.* Chicago: Rand McNally, 1973.
3. BSCS. *Biological Science: An Inquiry Into Life.* New York: Harcourt, Brace, Jovanovich, 1973.
4. Payne, C. and Falls, W. *Modern Physical Science.* Dubuque, Iowa: W.C. Brown Co., 1974.
5. Pella, M. *Physical Science for Progress.* Englewood Cliffs, New Jersey: Prentice-Hall, 1970.
6. Ramsey, W. and others. *Modern Earth Science.* New York: Holt, Rinehart, and Winston, 1969.
7. Tracy, G. and others. *Modern Physical Science.* New York: Holt, Rinehart, and Winston, 1970.

ACKNOWLEDGMENTS

The author wishes to thank those people who helped in the preparation of this text:

Cathy Nelson who read and typed the original manuscript.

Karyl Gatteno and John Black who took the photographs.

Pranthana Konsupto for UNICEF photo and Vicki Pierce for photo on page 67.

Snowrene Saxton and Joan Nason who made many helpful suggestions during the field testing of the extra activities.

Instructional Media Center, Essex Community College, Baltimore, Maryland.

Orange Coast College, Costa Mesa, California.

Arbor Hill Day Care Center, Albany, New York.

Candy Cane Lane Day Care Center, Albany, New York.

Kinder Lane Preschool and Day Nursery, Albany, New York.

The following members of the staff at Delmar Publishers contributed to this publication:

Director of Publications: Alan N. Knofla
Series Editor: Elinor Gunnerson
Source Editor: Judith Barrow
Copy Editor: Diana Miller

All of the material for this manuscript was classroom tested at Forest Home Avenue School, Milwaukee, Wisconsin, in a class of three- and four-year-olds. Selected portions of the text were also tested at the Twelfth Street School, Milwaukee, Wisconsin.

INDEX

379 (8C854)